AARP®

500 Great Ways to Save

by The Experts at AARP

for **dummies®**

A Wiley Brand

500 Great Ways to Save For Dummies®

Contents at a Glance

Table of Contents

Introduction

As prices climb for nearly everything, from food to gas to healthcare and beyond, what can you do to spend less and save more? That's where *500 Great Ways to Save For Dummies* comes in. Here, experts reveal simple, secret, and successful ways to get more for your money. Taking off from "99 Great Ways to Save," the *AARP Bulletin's* most popular annual series published each July, we asked experts in their field for their top tips — and they told us.

About This Book

500 Great Ways to Save For Dummies is chock-full of ideas for slashing expenses in a variety of categories, including cars, clothes, technology, pets, entertainment, education, fitness, and much more. You'll discover loads of insider tips for finding freebies. And experts offer pointers on turning around your personal finances and making the most of your long-term investments. Plus you'll find handy apps and websites that can help you save big bucks!

But be a cautious consumer. While most websites and apps highlighted in this book are free, not all are. Check the fine print. And beware of privacy policies of any websites where you provide sensitive information. Also be cautious when using apps.

Here are eight tips for app safety:

1. Download from well-known app stores such as the app store on your smartphone.

2. Read reviews and ratings. Only download apps that are highly rated, have been well reviewed by multiple users, and have been around for more than a few weeks or months.

3. Read the terms and conditions and as much of the privacy policy as possible.

4. Never give out your passwords.

5. Don't grant remote access.

6. Avoid clicking ads.

7. Avoid giving apps access to your contacts.

8. Ask yourself if you really need the app.

In this book, you may note that some web addresses break across two lines of text. If you're reading this book in print and want to visit one of these web pages, simply key in the address exactly as it's noted in the text, as though the line break doesn't exist. If you're reading this text as an e-book, you've got it easy — just click the address to be taken directly to the page.

Foolish Assumptions

This book assumes that you want to keep more of your hard-earned money in your pocket, whether the economy is contracting or booming. You can find help in these pages if you want to do any of the following:

>> Get into a saving mindset even as prices rise.

>> Figure out your finances and prepare a budget.

>> Eliminate debt.

>> Cut car, home maintenance, and utility costs.

>> Save on food, healthcare, fitness, and other regular expenses as well as major purchases.

>> Go out on the town, pursue hobbies, and care for pets without breaking the bank.

>> Travel far and near without going into debt.

Icons Used in This Book

Icons are those fun drawings you see in the page margins now and again. Here's what they mean.

This icon highlights money-saving benefits that are available to AARP members. *Note:* Please note that AARP discounts may change; we highlight those in effect when we went to press. If the URL is no longer active, or if you're interested in even more discounts, visit aarp.org and search "member benefits," or if you're already a member, browse aarp.org/memberdiscounts.

MILITARY & VETERANS

Find deals specifically for active military and veterans marked with this icon.

OLDER ADULTS

If you're 65 or older — whether or not you're an AARP member! — you can save big bucks on tips designated with this icon.

STUDENTS

Are you a student or do you have a student in your life? Discover discounts meant for students with this icon.

Where to Go from Here

You don't have to read this book from cover to cover, but feel free to do so! If you just want to find tips in a specific subject, take a look at the table of contents or the index, and then dive into the chapter or section that interests you. For example:

>> Want to slash your food bills? Start with Chapter 2.

>> Eager to become a savvy shopper, even when you're making major purchases? Check out Chapters 6, 7, and 8.

>> Don't know how to save money on healthcare and insurance? Chapter 9 shows you the way.

>> Looking to enjoy fun stuff like going out, hosting parties, and celebrating holidays for less? Get the scoop in Chapters 11 and 16.

>> Interested in strengthening your personal finances and investing for the long term? You'll find lots of pointers in Chapters 18 and 19.

No matter what the economy is doing, saving money never goes out of style. Find ways to save on practically everything! And if you want even more tips, check out the *AARP Bulletin's* "99 Great Ways to Save," published each July.

Chapter **1**

Managing Your Money

A budget is the first step to living within your means and, even more important, living the life you choose. Knowing your expenses, your income, and your financial goals is the foundation. In this chapter, we ask you to grab a notebook — or create an easy spreadsheet on your computer — to find out just where you stand financially so that you can move forward with financial awareness and stability.

We start by taking a look at expenses. How much do you spend each month? What are fixed expenses — those bills you pay regularly? What about variable expenses — those that fluctuate? Think about the difference between basic necessities and luxuries — needs versus wants.

Next, we look at income. How much do you earn? Do you have investments? Other streams of income? If you're older, do you have retirement income?

Plus, we set our sights on the future. What are your financial goals? Going out to dinner more often? Fixing the roof? Visiting family more often or going on that dream vacation?

These are the types of questions you look at in this chapter. And, with the answers to these questions, you can begin to create a budget. When you become financially aware, your life can change in ways small and big. You can make room for things that matter so you're living life on your terms.

Seeing Where Your Money Goes: Your Expenses

Tracking your expenses for a month or longer can show you exactly where your money is going. Write down what you spend in cash, by check, and through payment services such as CashApp, PayPal, and Venmo. Review your debit and credit card expenditures. Then look at periodic — including quarterly and annual — expenditures such as taxes, homeowners or renters insurance, and vacations. You'll most likely discover spending patterns, some of which may surprise you. Perhaps you realize you're spending way too much in a category, like takeout meals or multiple streaming services. Or maybe you find that your medications are depleting your income, and you want to look at discount cards or different insurance options.

Identifying fixed expenses

Fixed expenses are approximately the same amount of money every billing period, such as your rent or mortgage and car payments. Fixed expenses are paid weekly, monthly, quarterly, or annually. For example, you may pay for your car registration every year or two and your car insurance monthly or quarterly. Weekly fixed expenses may include things like a parking or commuter pass. Figure 1-1 shows various examples of fixed expenses.

Fixed Expenses

Housing

- Rent
- Mortgage
- Property taxes
- Homeowners association or condo fees
- Internet
- Electricity
- Water
- Landline
- Gas
- Lawn maintenance

Insurance

- Disability insurance
- Health insurance
- Life insurance
- Renters or homeowners insurance
- Vehicle insurance

Medical

- Flexible spending account
- High-yield savings account

Work

- Public transportation
- Parking
- Professional association fees

Personal

- Gym and other memberships
- Newspaper and magazine subscriptions
- Streaming services
- Cellphone
- Car payments
- House of worship

Children

- Childcare
- Tuition
- 529 and Coverdell savings accounts
- After-school activities

FIGURE 1-1: Spending categories that are considered fixed expenses.

Allowing for variable expenses

Variable expenses, or *variable costs,* unlike fixed expenses, vary from month to month and may be items you regularly purchase or ones you buy only occasionally (see Figure 1-2). Common variable expenses include areas like the following:

>> Groceries

>> Gas for your car

>> Food for your pets

>> Items for any hobbies

>> Personal care items like hygiene products or makeup

Variable Expenses

Food

- Groceries
- Dining out
- Lunch (work and school)
- Coffee

Transportation

- Gas
- Tolls
- Oil changes and other maintenance
- Car repairs
- Bus and train fare
- Parking

Leisure

- Concerts
- Movies and museums
- Books
- Hobbies
- Games for family
- Vacations

Household

- Pet food and supplies
- Veterinary care
- Cleaning supplies
- Decor
- Home maintenance and repairs

Miscellaneous

- Clothing
- Haircuts
- Charitable contributions
- Gifts
- Medical co-pays and out-of-pocket expenses
- Sports, lessons, tutors, school field trips

FIGURE 1-2: Spending categories that are variable expenses.

These types of expenses can be more challenging for you to track. Depending on the time of year or stage of your life, your spending in these categories can fluctuate. You may spend nearly nothing in a category like household items one month and then easily spend a few hundred dollars there the next month. You may spend a lot more money during the holiday season between vacations and gifts.

Once you've tracked variable expenses for a few months, you'll have an easier time assigning a monetary value to them. A category may occasionally spike, initially throwing everything you had planned off course. You're going to figure this all out.

Calculating your total spending

Now you're ready to evaluate what you spend every month. Grab your notebook or open up your spreadsheet and follow these steps:

1. Make a list of your fixed expenses.

In addition to your housing expenses, list car payments and fun things like gym memberships, subscription boxes, and streaming services. Divide these into categories. For instance, under housing you'd put mortgage or rent, homeowners or renters insurance, and utilities.

2. Make a list of your variable expenses.

Just as you did for fixed expenses, put your variable expenses in categories.

3. Add up the total monthly costs for fixed expenses each month.

You now clearly see how much you spend every month on your fixed expenses. Once you've done this for a few months, compare your fixed expenses month over month.

4. Add up the total annual costs for variable expenses.

Because these are periodic, not monthly, you'll need to gather your expenses over time to see your annual costs. To get a monthly estimate, divide by 12.

5. Evaluate whether you need those expenses.

Consider whether all your expenses are necessary. Do you need to spend money on a gym membership every month, or can you find a cheaper way to work out, such as walking on local trails? If you've signed up to get monthly items or deliveries, do you have the option to pause them and work through your current supply instead?

Assess your larger expenses, too — not just the minor ones. For example: You realize rent may be costing you more of your take-home pay than you're comfortable with. Moving can be expensive, but make a note to research other living arrangements when you get closer to the end of your lease.

Understanding needs versus wants

Fixed and variable expenses can include both needs and wants:

>> Generally speaking, *needs* include categories such as rent or mortgage payments, food, gas to get to and from work if you commute, and health care, including medicine.

>> *Wants* are things like eating out, getting a new cellphone when your current one works fine, and going to concerts and movies.

Consider ways to save on both needs and wants. For instance, on needs, look for weekly specials at the grocery store. For wants, find deals at the cosmetic counter.

The difference between needs and wants can get murky quickly, especially because one person's want may genuinely be another person's need. Spending money on your wants is perfectly okay; you just need to figure out how to budget for them.

Be realistic when determining your wants and needs. Suppose you have a specific life situation that requires you to spend a bit more on your variable expenses. If so, budget for it. Perhaps you have a busy, stressful job. Maybe getting a massage once a month and ordering takeout a few times a week makes your own and your family's life manageable. Perhaps you pay more in a specific category, like eating out, than people say you should. But being realistic about your spending will help keep you on budget.

Knowing Where Your Money Comes From: Your Income

Your *income* is an essential component of your budget. Knowing how much money you have coming in helps you make sure your expenses don't exceed your income. It can also help you set realistic goals for all areas that relate to your finances and perhaps even quality of life. When tracking your income, you may realize you have more than you initially thought you had. On the other hand, when you look at your income and expenses, you may find you have a spending deficit, which means you need to find ways to either cut back or earn more.

When discussing your work income, one dollar amount you need to keep in mind is your *net pay*. Net pay is the amount of money left after any withholdings you may be subjected to, such as federal and state taxes, FICA taxes (supporting Social Security and Medicare), health insurance, and any wage garnishments you may be paying off. Your net pay is the money you have to pay your fixed and variable expenses and put toward savings and your goals.

Your income may also include earnings from your investments and other sources such as, if you're older, retirement income.

Depending on a monthly income

The first type of income you should consider is what you earn monthly to cover all your expenses. *Monthly income* can come from various sources. While it can be consistent, it can also be different from month to month. Here's a list of different types of monthly income you can earn:

>> **Income from full-time and/or part-time employment:** This is income you receive from an employer that has you on its payroll. Some jobs pay a *salary* — a flat amount of money per paycheck — and others pay an hourly *wage*. Unlike a salary, hourly income can fluctuate because the number of hours you work may vary.

>> **Income as a self-employed freelancer or consultant:** Freelancers and contractors are considered self-employed, but the main difference is that *freelancers* generally balance more than one client and work on projects with a short timeline. *Contractors* often work with one main client on a longer time frame. (For tax purposes, there is no distinction between the two.)

>> **Pensions and other paid retirement plans:** A *pension* is a type of retirement program that an employee, an employer, or both pay into. The plan pays a fixed sum to the employee at regular intervals upon retirement. Some pensions require you to work for the company for a certain number of years before you're eligible (or *vested*). Federal, state, and local government or other public sectors also allow for paid retirement plans.

>> **Self-funded retirement plans:** Outside of traditional pensions or government-paid retirement plans, you may receive payments from retirement accounts, such as 401(k)s, 403(b)s, and IRAs. These types of retirement accounts allow you to save for retirement by investing.

>> **Social Security retirement benefits:** When people talk about receiving Social Security, they're usually referring to retirement benefits. Every year you remain in the workforce, you can receive up to four work credits. After you've earned 40 credits, you're eligible to collect benefits. When you can start receiving Social Security retirement benefits depends on when you were born. The longer you wait to receive benefits, up to age 70, the larger your payments. For up-to-date information, visit www.ssa.gov/retirement or see AARP's *Social Security For Dummies.*

>> **Social Security Disability Benefits, Supplemental Security Income, and survivors benefits:** Social Security has three other benefits. If you're disabled, you can receive two different types of benefits.

- *Social Security Disability Insurance (SSDI)* benefits are granted when you meet the Social Security Administration's definition of having a disability and you have earned enough workforce credits, depending on the age you become disabled.

- If you've never worked due to a disability, you can qualify for *Supplemental Security Income (SSI).*

Last but not least, if you're a child, spouse, or parent who relies on someone in the workforce to support you and that person dies, you may be eligible for *survivors benefits.*

You can create a Social Security account at www.ssa.gov/myaccount. Doing so allows you to check your workforce credits and the money you've paid into Social Security and to get an estimate of your retirement benefit payment. You can also check to see what other Social Security benefits may be available to you, such as disability insurance or survivors benefits, along with the amount you or a loved one would qualify for. This information can help you budget better for life circumstances and save for retirement.

>> **Cash benefits from the state:** You may qualify for cash assistance in some states, depending on your situation. Temporary Assistance for Needy Families (TANF) is one example. Along with cash assistance, other benefits you may be eligible for are work assistance, specific training to enter back into the workforce, and help with childcare. Find out more at www.benefits.gov/benefit/613.

You Gotta Have Dreams: Financial Goals

You'll want to set aside money for emergency expenses. But you'll also want to set financial goals. Goals can be simple, like going to a concert once a month. They can be moderate, like treating the family for dinner every Sunday or saving enough so you can retire comfortably. They can also be ambitious, like taking a dream vacation. After you're clear on your financial goals, figuring out the steps to get you there is easier.

Setting financial goals can help you live a better quality of life, which can mean the difference in where you can afford to live, what you do in your free time, whether you can take a leave of absence due to a life-changing emergency, and when you can retire.

Saving for your future

Life is short, and putting money aside for your future sets you up for long-term financial security — and happiness. In addition to retirement accounts, you may need a new car for transportation to and from work. Maybe the perfect home of your dreams hits the housing market, and you see yourself establishing some roots! You may have kids or grandkids heading off to college — or you may want to go back to school yourself to make more money so you can have an even sounder budget than before. Somedays can turn into your current day, so you may as well plan for them.

Saving for the future can also include fabulous trips you want to experience, like sightseeing in Europe or wine tasting in Napa. Maybe it's establishing a scholarship fund in someone's name at a local nonprofit, redecorating your house, or buying a muscle car to restore. Your future needs to include fun, and your budget helps you do just that.

Make sure your goal is actually yours. You may hear, for example, that the way to make the most money is to become your own boss. It may not be as easy as some people claim. Many people quit their jobs to become entrepreneurs but don't have a clear plan or realize they aren't suited for self-employment at all. Make sure whatever financial goal you choose is one that you want to achieve, so you'll put in the hard work to make it your reality.

Paying down your debt

Another financial goal you may want to set is paying down your debt. Debt isn't evil if you use it strategically. But having even strategic debt can cost thousands of dollars in interest and financing fees. Setting a financial goal to pay your debt down, no matter how slowly, can help in the long run. Because as soon as you pay off that debt, you have more cash flow to do things that are important to you.

Putting your financial goals in place

Setting financial goals doesn't have to be complicated. Just follow these steps:

1. **Establish what your goals are.**

For example, maybe you want to buy a house.

2. **Make the goal as clear as can be.**

Decide precisely how much money you'll need to buy that house and when you want to be able to make the purchase.

3. **Take actionable steps toward completing it.**

Examples of actionable steps may be slowly paying off your credit card so that eventually you can open a high-yield savings account for the house you want. Every little bit adds up, so don't be discouraged if you have to start small. With every action, you move the needle closer to your goal.

Creating Your Budget

After you've set out your expenses, income, and financial goals, it's time to put it all together. In your notebook or on your spreadsheet, you've set out your three components:

>> Expenses (how much money you spend), both fixed and variable

>> Income (how much money comes in)

>> Financial goals (things you want to accomplish, such as retiring, paying down debt, and saving for something in the future)

Now you probably see that all three are equally important. Your expenses can affect how much income you need to bring in, which determines whether you can accomplish your goals by working one regular full-time job or also getting a side gig. Your income determines how much money you can spend on your lifestyle or put toward your future, like vacations or retirement. It's all related, so the sooner you figure out what you need to pay and what you want to accomplish, the faster a budget will work for you.

Add up your income and subtract your expenses. Perhaps as you see your budget in full, you realize your net pay doesn't cover all your monthly expenses or the goals you've set for yourself. In these cases, you have to either cut your spending or increase your income.

Finding ways to cut your expenses

Here are some ideas—and you'll find 500 more in later chapters!

>> See whether you can get a better rate by paying for certain things, like insurance, annually rather than monthly.

>> Call your providers, such as cellphone or internet, to see whether you qualify for any discounts or loyalty rates. Sometimes saying that you're preparing to move to another provider will prompt the offer of a discount.

>> Research competitors for insurance policies: healthcare, automobile, renters or homeowners, and life.

>> Consider switching to different tiers of subscription services, such as home streaming networks.

>> Discuss options with your landlord or mortgage company.

Nothing is off the table; the more money you can free up, the more you have to save for your goals or spend on things that bring value to your life.

Identifying additional sources of income

The economy can be volatile. A job may be here one day and out-sourced the next. Or your needs and circumstances can change. This section offers a few ways you can earn additional income.

Earning rental income

Renting a room is a common way to break even on your living expenses. Collecting the monthly payment from a roommate is considered rental income. You can also earn rental income if you're a landlord or have investment properties you collect earnings on.

Another way people earn this type of income is by renting their residences as short-term vacation rentals. With websites such as Airbnb and VRBO, you can rent out a room in your home or the entire house for a nightly fee.

Taking part-time gigs

You can earn extra income by doing odd jobs or selling stuff. Here are some common side hustles:

>> Shop and deliver groceries or restaurant meals.

>> Sell items you have laying around or buy items for a lower price and then sell them for a profit on sites like Amazon, eBay, and Facebook Marketplace.

>> Create content online as a writer.

>> Make crafts and sell them on a site like Etsy, Handmade Artists, Facebook Marketplace, or other social media.

>> Put together furniture.

>> Babysit kids.

>> Be a companion for older people.

>> Dog-walk and pet sit, either at your house or theirs.

>> Drive for rideshare services.

Setting aside money for taxes

Income from side gigs may be considered earned income depending on the source, so check with the IRS to see whether you need to put money aside for taxes. If so, save 25 to 30 percent of any income earned from side hustles in a checking account. Pay your estimated taxes quarterly and save anything left over for business expenses. You may be able to deduct certain expenses on your taxes. For more information on self-employment taxes, visit www.irs.gov.

Like anything in life that you're trying to improve, things may feel uncomfortable in the beginning. Finding out you spend far more than you earn, for example, can be discouraging. But keep this in mind: Knowing your expenses and income and creating a realistic budget can have a cascading effect and improve all areas of your life.

Celebrate the small wins, and know your future is more financially stable every day.

Slashing Your Food Bill

To save money on food, whether eating at home or out, we asked our experts for their top savings tips. Here's what they told us.

Saving at the Grocery Store

1. Check out mygrocerydeals.com and flipp.com, where you can compare sale prices in your local supermarkets.

OLDER ADULTS

2. Some grocery stores and chains offer older and student shoppers unadvertised discounts of up to 10 percent. The savings are typically available only on slow midweek shopping days. Local stores, regional chains, and co-ops are more likely to offer the discounts than national chains. Ask at your store, or search "grocery stores" and "senior discount" or "student discount."

3. Sign up for your local supermarkets' loyalty programs, which let you get cheaper prices for some items. And clip store coupons. Most grocery stores have taken their coupons online, making it easy to download them onto your card before you leave home.

4. Tap into SNAP. Formerly known as food stamps, the Supplemental Nutrition Assistance Program provides eligible individuals with monthly benefits to purchase groceries at participating supermarkets and farmers markets. To be eligible, your monthly income must be less than 130 percent of the U.S. poverty line.

   Visit AARP Foundation at aarp.org/aarp-foundation/ our-work/food-security/ for guidance or benefits.gov/ benefit/361 to apply.

5. Weigh prepackaged produce. Not every 10-pound bag of potatoes is created equal. The weight marked is the minimum required by law, so use the scale to find the best buy.

6. If you need only a few vegetables or fruits for a recipe or meal, buying a small amount at the supermarket salad bar may be cheaper than buying a bag of whole or precut vegetables.

7. Stock your freezer with fruits and veggies. Prices for fresh fruits and vegetables are volatile. Costs for frozen produce can be more stable. Check the circulars or your store's loyalty app for sales in the freezer aisle. Then buy in bulk. It's just as healthy: Producers freeze vegetables and fruits at peak freshness, locking in nutrients.

8. Scoop your own rice and beans. Bulk bins are popular in many food stores. You could pay less for every ounce of beans, grains, and rice that you scoop on your own into a bag.

9. To combat higher costs, manufacturers sometimes shrink their package sizes or grow their packaging, giving consumers less for the same price. For packaged goods, such as toilet paper, snacks, and cereal, check the unit cost displayed at most grocers, and don't be fooled by new packaging. It could just be hiding less.

10. Experts say you want organic fruits or veggies when you're eating the whole thing. But skip organic for bananas, oranges, avocadoes, and other foods you peel.

11. As food prices surge, usual strategies like clipping coupons can help stretch your dollars. But you can take your savings to another level if you're open to what's known as "salvage food."

Salvage food is the stuff regular supermarkets pass on — items such as cosmetically flawed produce, dented cans, crumpled boxes, and products nearing expiration dates.

Not all those rejects end up in landfills. Some turn up on supermarket clearance racks and at salvage grocery stores. And the Flashfood smartphone app lets you buy discounted food nearing its "best by" date at traditional grocers, including Giant, Martin's, and Meijer. Here's a quick overview of your salvage food options.

- **Salvage grocery stores:** Visit the website buysalvagefood.com to find salvage stores near you. Before buying, check items for problems such as mold on cheese and food that's far past its expiration date. Grocery Outlet operates 420 stores, mostly in the Western United States; United Grocery Outlet, a different company, has three dozen stores in six Southern states. Many smaller salvage grocers operate around the country. Sites such as Hungry Harvest, Imperfect Foods, and Misfits Market offer home delivery of salvage foods. Imperfect Foods and Misfits Market both focus on organic products; all the food is high-quality, but prices are close to those of Whole Foods. (Misfits Market acquired Imperfect Foods in late 2022 but operates it as a separate brand.)

- **Supermarket clearance racks:** At some grocery stores you can find "scratch and dent" racks — shelves usually in the back of stores — with big markdowns. Don't worry about smashed boxes as long as the inner bag is sealed. Minor dings in a can are okay, but dents that are deep or along a can's seams can signal dangerous bacteria.

- **Salvage food-delivery websites:** Visit https://build myharvest.com/, imperfectfoods.com, and misfits market.com to see if they deliver in your area.

Tip: Check for deals at grocery stores near you through the Flashfood app. The selection may be more limited than those of the delivery services, but the savings are worth it.

12. Cruise the periphery. Fresh produce, dairy foods, and bulk grains are often cheaper — and more nutritious — than the packaged foods in the middle of the store.

13. Go all-in on store brands. Many major grocery chains have greatly expanded their store-brand lines, and their reputation for quality has improved. Chains are highly secretive about who makes their products, but some generic products may be manufactured by the same company that puts out the name-brand version. Simply compare the ingredients list with name-brand versions to see how close they are. Generic brands can run as much as 25 percent less than the name-brand version.

14. Bring your own bags. In a growing number of communities, you'll pay 5 to 10 cents a bag. You could easily save $25 a year.

15. Keep your eyes glued to the register at checkout and review your receipt to spot errors. Some stores even have a "scan guarantee policy," which means you get the item for free or at a discount if the price the register displays is higher than the real price.

**MILITARY &
VETERANS**

16. Check for military and veterans discounts at your grocery, big-box, and specialty stores on Veterans Day and year round. Find discounts for national chains at military.com/discounts/groceries.

17. Shop less to save more. Food shoppers spend about 50 percent more than they planned because of impulse buys, researchers say. Restricting yourself to one weekly trip instead of three could save you hundreds of dollars a year.

18. Every three months, most supermarket products go on sale and brand-name coupons appear online or in the newspaper. That's food for thought to help you know when to stock up. Other sales occur during promotions like National Ice Cream Month and National Hot Dog Month — both in July.

19. Yes, order online. It can save you money by avoiding impulse purchases when browsing a store. Here are more ways to save when ordering online:

- **Cut your delivery costs.** Watch for free and discounted delivery at your local stores, and search for newspaper or store coupons to find deals, such as $20 off your first order at Vons, 15 percent off Kroger grocery shipments, and $10 off your first delivery of $20 at Instacart.

- **Opt for pickup.** Some stores let you order online and pick up at the store. This saves you time (your bags will be packed and ready to go), the delivery fee, and maybe a tip.

- **Get loyalty rewards.** Some supermarkets don't let you use your loyalty card with online orders. So if you have a choice, opt for stores that do, such as Albertsons, Giant, and Kroger.

- **Avoid pricey substitutes.** If items you order are out of stock, stores sometimes substitute costlier alternatives, which raises your bill. Ask to be contacted to approve any replacements. You don't want the store to substitute without your okay an expensive brand-name product for a lower-cost generic you ordered. If something like this happens to you, complain and ask for a credit on your next order.

Making Your Money Go Further

20. Americans throw away 30 to 40 percent of our food supply, often because it goes uneaten until it's no longer edible. The antidote: Cook at least one meal a week based entirely on foods lingering in your refrigerator or pantry. Make Thursday "pantry cooking" night.

21. Have an "eat me first" spot in your fridge. Designate a shelf or bin in your fridge for all the leftover food bits (think nubs of cheese, a half serving of pasta, a lemon wedge) or overly ripe foodstuffs that should be eaten before fresher items.

22. Eat meatless at least once a week. Three ground-beef burgers cost an estimated $5.69, but you can make three veggie burgers from a 99-cent can of beans.

23. With store-bought salad dressing costing $2.99 or more, why not make your own? A vinaigrette is 2 tablespoons wine vinegar, 2 teaspoons Dijon mustard, ½ teaspoon salt, ⅓ cup olive oil, and pepper to taste.

24. Plan this Friday for next Tuesday. A proven way to contain grocery costs is to plan out the week's meals and to buy food from a shopping list based solely on that plan. Friday is a great day for planning, as many stores post their week's discounts and deals that day or the day before.

25. Prolong the life of your fruits and veggies. Wrap them with a paper towel and put them into a container or plastic bag. The towel will absorb water that causes rot. And line the produce drawer with paper towels.

Wash produce right before you use it, not as soon as you bring it home. Washing fruits and vegetables before you store them can make them spoil faster because of their damp skin. Plus, bacteria can grow on produce while it's stored in your refrigerator.

Shopping in Bulk

26. Cross items off your weekly list by buying in bulk, locking in the low price for months. Watch for steep markdowns on canned foods, butter, cereal, pasta, and olive oil.

27. Get your favorite brew for less. If you love a particular coffee at a local coffee shop, buy some in bulk so you can brew it at home. To keep it fresh, portion it into smaller bags and squeeze out as much air as you can before sealing. Store the bags in the freezer.

28. Get wine by the case. Most wine stores will take at least 10 percent off your purchase if you walk out with 12 bottles. You could save $48 on two cases of $20 wine, and you'll always have a gift ready when you visit someone.

29. Use big-box stores — but use them wisely. Prices on most products will be lower than regular grocery store prices, but know your prices and watch out for impulse buying. If you know you can buy bananas at your grocery store for 59 cents a pound, for example, you won't be so easily lured by the three-pound bunch for $1.99.

Finally, split your membership with a friend to halve your annual fee, and split your purchases, too. It may be hard for you to eat five pounds of peaches before they spoil, but if you divide the purchase among friends, you avoid throwing out unused food.

**MILITARY &
VETERANS**

30. At BJ's Wholesale Club and Sam's Club, veterans can get a discount on new memberships, while Costco gives vets a $20 Costco Shop Card when they join. Visit your local store or their websites for details.

Eating Out

31. AARP members can get up to 15 percent off at national chains such as Denny's, Jamba, McAlister's Deli, Moe's Southwest Grill, and Outback Steakhouse, plus find discounts for local restaurants. Visit aarp.org/restaurant-discounts.

32. Many restaurants, such as Chick-fil-A, Domino's, McDonald's, Papa John's, and Wendy's, offer discounts when the area's professional sports teams win. Look for a promo code to use when ordering by phone or online.

**OLDER
ADULTS**

33. Bring your ID! Ask restaurants if they have a discount for older or student diners. At 15 percent off, you could save $7.50 on a $50 dinner for two.

34. Eat out for lunch instead of dinner. Lunch entrees and appetizers are typically 25 percent to 50 percent cheaper than dinner items, and the portions are sometimes just as big. Breakfast is even cheaper.

**MILITARY &
VETERANS**

35. To honor those who serve or have served in the military, many restaurants offer free and discounted meals, especially on Veterans Day. For a list, visit veteran.com/military-discounts.

36. Many restaurants and quick-serve establishments will help you celebrate your birthday by giving you a discount on menu items, a free drink, or even a birthday dessert. The days of simply saying it's your birthday to get a freebie are largely over. Most restaurants require you to sign up for their loyalty program to get the celebratory kickback. These deals tend to be good for a few days after your birthday, which means you can spread out the savings.

37. If you are asked to take a survey at the end of the meal, do it. Sometimes restaurants will reward you with a coupon or discount for sharing your thoughts on your experience.

Tech to Save You Money

38. Double up with cash-back apps. With services like Coupons. com, Fetch Rewards, or Ibotta, your grocery purchases earn points toward cash back or gift cards for various shopping options such as Amazon, Target, and Walmart. Fetch Rewards, for example, has a section where you can see which brands will get you the most points.

39. Search before you shop. Flipp is a free phone app that consolidates retail circulars. The Weekly Ad (www.theweeklyad.com) offers the same service online. This makes it a snap to compare your shopping list to circulars from your local supermarkets to determine which store's virtual coupons will save you the most money. You can also use the Flipp app to generate your shopping list.

40. Try the FoodKeeper app. The USDA offers a free mobile app for Apple and Android users that provides information on how to best store over 400 food and beverage items. It also offers an option to log your purchases and receive notifications when your food is about to expire. Find the FoodKeeper app at foodsafety.gov/keep-food-safe/foodkeeper-app.

41. Search for restaurant discounts at groupon.com, living social.com, and restaurant.com. For example, you could pay $10 for a $25 gift certificate — and save $15 on a night out.

Cashing In on Car Savings

Whether you're driving across town or across the country, buying a new or used car, or looking to lower your insurance premiums, these tips from our top experts can help you save a few cents here, a few hundred and even thousand dollars there. (Find tips on rental cars in the later section on vacations and travel.)

Saving on Gas

42. Buy gas on Mondays. It's the cheapest gas day in most states, according to a study by GasBuddy (www.gasbuddy.com).

43. Cross state lines for gas. Prices vary mostly due to different tax rates. Check GasBuddy, gasprices.aaa.com, Geico, or Waze if you're planning an interstate drive or live close to a state border.

44. When you link your Exxon Mobil Rewards+ account to your AARP membership, you earn extra points on fuel and convenience store items. Learn how at aarp.org/exxon-benefit.

45. Use gas advantage programs. Many grocery store chains, including Giant (https://giantfood.com/rewards-overview), Kroger (www.kroger.com/d/fuel-points-program), and Safeway (www.safeway.com/foru/program-details.html), let you earn a discount at select gas stations.

46. When you've finished filling your gas tank and the pump has shut off, invert the pump nozzle 180 degrees while it's still in the fill hole. There's an extra ounce or two of gasoline in there — which you already paid for!

47. Check your cap. An estimated 17 percent of the cars on the road have a broken, loose, or missing gasoline cap. This allows your gasoline to vaporize, hurting your mileage and harming the environment.

48. Be a chill driver. Hard braking, quick acceleration, and speeding can lower your gas mileage by 30 to 40 percent.

49. Keep your windows closed when driving on the highway over 55 miles per hour. Open windows can reduce your gas mileage by as much as 10 percent. In stop-and-go traffic, save gas by opening the windows and turning off the air conditioning.

50. When it's safe, turn off your engine when idling. Just 10 seconds of idling your car's engine uses as much gas as restarting it. Two minutes uses enough fuel to drive a mile.

Extending the Life of Your Car

51. Ignore that oil-change sticker. Most oil-change shops slap a sticker on your windshield summoning you back in 3,000 miles. Check your owner's manual. Many newer cars use a synthetic oil that needs changing far less frequently than older cars.

52. Save 15 percent off drive-through, stay-in-your-car oil changes — including a free 18-point maintenance check. The discount also applies toward preventive maintenance services, including radiator, air filter or wiper blade replacements, and transmission and differential services. Visit aarp.org/valvoline-benefit.

53. Get no- or low-cost service at auto parts stores. If you buy windshield wipers or a battery at an auto parts store and have trouble installing them yourself, the sales staff may be willing to install them for you, often for far less than a service shop would charge.

54. Rotate tires for free. Many tire stores will rotate tires you bought there at no cost. Plus, some brands include free rotation for the life of the tires at any authorized dealer. Just call to set up a time and verify that there's no cost.

55. Empty your trunk. Most of us know what it feels like to be hauling a few extra pounds around the midriff. It's no different with your car — excess weight places more demands on your engine and creates suspension, braking, and even exhaust problems.

Check your car right now. What's in there that can come out? Every pound counts.

56. Check engine belts. Broken belts are a major cause of breakdowns. Be sure to check yours — or have them checked — before you go on a long trip. Avoid one break-down and save in towing fees.

57. Compare, then repair. If time permits, get competitive bids for any major work done on your car. Get an online estimate from AAA (aaa.com/autorepair/estimate) or Consumer Reports (www.consumerreports.org/cars/car-repair-assistant). Then find searchable lists of repair shops at CarTalk.com, Consumer Reports (https://www.consumer reports.org/cars/car-repair-assistant/), and RepairPal.com. Want a house call? Search "mobile mechanics near me" or visit CarCareToGo, Wrench, or YourMechanic.com, which connect drivers to auto mechanics.

58. Cars aren't just transportation — they're a major investment. The average price of a new car in the United States was nearly $50,000 in January 2023. And while used car prices have started to level off, the average cost is still about $27,000.

So, keeping your car in top condition is both a good way to help avoid being forced to dive into the car market and a good way to increase its value if you do decide to trade up.

While a lot of car repairs require professionals, there are still plenty of ways to save money and do it yourself. The first stop for anyone considering a little automotive DIY should be online. There's no shortage of videos available for just about every imaginable automotive task. A lot of those videos will make it clear whether the repair is something for beginners or advanced garage mechanics.

Here are a few places on your car where a little DIY time will not only save you money but make your car both better and safer.

- **Revive your owner's manual.** Once a year, pull out that manual and get refreshed answers to every relevant question you can come up with. What service should I be getting? How do I operate the car if my key fob dies? What does that dashboard light mean?

- **Clean your engine.** Do this to easily spot the source of any leaks, should they arise. Clean the engine at least a couple of times a year by spraying with a commercial engine degreaser and then rinsing with a garden hose.

- **Buy new wiper blades.** Make sure you buy the right length of blade, since the passenger's and driver's sides often use blades of different lengths. Typically, no tools are necessary, but watch carefully how the old one pops out. It will make installing the new one easier.

- **"Check Engine" light on? You've got this.** Get an onboard diagnostics (OBD 2) scanner at an auto parts store (starting around $20). Plug it into the OBD port under the dash, usually on the driver's side. Look up the displayed code on the internet to learn whether you have a problem that requires a mechanic's attention — or just a loose gas cap.

- **Save your seats.** Small upholstery tears will eventually become big upholstery tears. If the interior is cloth, a needle and thread may do the trick. For leather or vinyl, you'll need to buy a car-seat patch kit; these run $10 and up.

- **Fix the fog.** There are plenty of kits to buff away headlight cloudiness on the market. You can also find DIY solutions online, including using toothpaste or baking soda as a cleaner.

- **Scrub your battery.** Battery corrosion is like a cancer under your car's hood. Once a year, you should check the terminals. If there's white or blue-green buildup, remove the connecting cables, mix some baking soda and water, pour it on the terminal, and start scrubbing. Be sure to wear gloves and eye protection.

- **Refresh your air filter.** Your engine air filter used to sit on the top of your engine. Now it's tucked away in some corner of the engine compartment with a plastic cover and fasteners. It's worth consulting your owner's manual to find it. Changing it yourself every 15,000 to 30,000 miles is one of the easiest ways to save yourself some money.

- **Air up.** Few car maintenance tasks are as important as maintaining proper tire pressure. It helps tires last longer, improves fuel mileage, and makes your car safer to drive. The suggested pressure is noted on the tires or on the driver's-side doorframe. At-home tire inflater air compressors start at around $30.

- **Touch up the exterior.** Have a few chips or scrapes in your paint? Determine your car's precise color; ask a dealer if necessary. Then buy touch-up paint from the dealer or an online retailer. Plenty of online videos can show you how to apply it.

Staying Safe and Protected

59. Take a safety course, online or in person, to learn proven driving techniques to help you keep safe on the road — and you may be eligible for a discount on car insurance. AARP offers a Smart Driver course. Visit www.aarp.org/auto/driver-safety/.

60. Consider pay-as-you-go insurance. A device installed in your car or an app on your smartphone records how much and how safely you drive and factors the results into your next insurance bill. Savings can be significant. Ask your insurance agent.

61. AARP's free Auto Buying Program can help you find your next safe new or used car. Shop online for vehicles with the safety features and technology designed to help keep you safe while driving. You don't have to be an AARP member to use the program, but AARP members who log in and purchase a new car will save at least $100 more than nonmembers who use the program.

Here's how it works: The program highlights top safety picks from the Insurance Institute for Highway Safety and shows what other people in your area recently paid for the car you're interested in purchasing, along with the car's market average price — all from your own home. If you agree to share your personal information with TrueCar and their Certified Dealers who have inventory that matches your search criteria, the AARP Auto Buying Program will reveal up-front price offers. After you select the best matches, local dealers will follow up with you by phone, email, and text. If you make a purchase from a Certified Dealer, report it via the program website within 45 days so you can take the AARP Smart Driver Online Course for free. Learn more at autobuying.aarp.org. (This website is not operated by AARP. A different privacy policy and terms of service will apply.)

62. Save up to 20 percent on annual membership fees for Allstate Roadside plans, including Roadside Assist and Roadside Elite. Upon enrollment, benefits include 24/7 towing, jump starts, tire changes, lockout assistance, and fuel delivery. Visit aarp.org/allstate-roadside.

Selling and Buying a Car

63. Sell your car privately. A private sale is likely to fetch more for your car than a dealer may pay for a trade-in. If you are buying a new car, negotiate that price independent of the trade-in; only after the deal is done should you let a dealer bid on your old car. That way you'll know what the dealer is really offering.

64. Get preapproved for a car loan. The interest rate from a local bank is often lower than at the dealership. Plus, the dealer will know you can easily go elsewhere, putting you in a better position to negotiate a lower price.

65. Shop late in the month. Salespeople may be scrambling to meet quotas for bonuses and be willing to share the wealth with you.

66. Yes, really, consider an electric vehicle (EV). Most major carmakers offer electric vehicles now, meaning prices are coming down while gas prices are going up. Increasingly, buying an electric vehicle is likely to make economic sense. Currently, if you drive 12,000 miles a year, you can probably expect to break even in about two to three years, versus a similar gas model. Some states offer incentives on certain EV models. Check out the U.S. Department of Energy's state-by-state breakdown at afdc.energy.gov/laws/state. EVs also have fewer moving parts than do their gas-powered relatives, with no pumping pistons, no complicated gear boxes, no fuel injectors, no radiators, and no crankshafts. And that means less maintenance and fewer repairs.

Public charging stations charge about twice what it costs to charge at home, so you'll save more if you drive mostly within the car's charge range. Apps are available to tell you where to find free public charging stations. As for home charging, you can plug in to a standard wall socket, although that experience will be slow, at a rate of just about 5 miles of range per hour. Installing higher-capacity wiring (costing as much as $1,800) can get you up to 250 miles of electricity during an overnight refuel.

67. Go to a dealership to test-drive cars you're interested in. But then *always* walk away and negotiate by phone or email once you've made a selection. You'll likely get a better deal and avoid tense hours of sitting across from a salesperson.

68. Consider Carvana (www.carvana.com) or CarMax (www.carmax.com) for your next vehicle purchase. There's no haggling involved, and your car may be delivered to your door. Plus, both companies offer a seven-day money-back guarantee.

69. Avoid extras when buying a new car. You can purchase floor mats at an auto store or online for less than a dealer charges. Fabric and paint treatments provide little protection for a lot of money. And vehicles come from the manufacturer with corrosion protection, making rust-proofing unnecessary.

MILITARY & VETERANS

70. Many car manufacturers offer new car discounts to military members, and some of them extend these offers to veterans. For a list, visit themilitarywallet.com/new-car-military-discounts/.

Tech to Save You Money

71. Check gas prices before you leave or on the road. Several phone apps provide the current cost of gas in the area where you're driving. For example, search "gas" on the Waze app, type "Geico gas" into your browser for the same result, or download the GasBuddy app. But keep in mind that if you wind up driving a lot more to save a few pennies, you can defeat the purpose of using the apps!

72. Consider a mileage app. Phone apps such as Mileage Tracker by Driversnote, Mileage Tracker by Everlance, and Stride: Mileage & Tax Tracker use your phone's GPS to track your business mileage and create reports. Free versions usually need to be started before each trip. If you drive a lot, it may be worth paying a few bucks monthly for a version that works automatically.

Saving Cold Cash on Utilities

Your number one money-saving task when it comes to utilities: In the winter, for instance, keep cold air outside and warm air inside by caulking and weather-stripping doors and windows. To do that, caulk and weather-strip doors and windows. Keep your fireplace flue tightly closed. Seal any air leaks where plumbing or electrical wiring comes through the walls. Then make sure your home is insulated properly. Find more tips on heating and cooling as well as water and electricity here.

Watching Water Costs

73. Fix that leaky toilet. That steady draining can waste 200 gallons per day and hundreds of dollars a year on your water bill! Some fixes are free (the chain might just be hung up). You can replace the whole mechanism for about $20.

74. Update every sink and tub with a new faucet or aerator marked with the WaterSense label. Aerators, which mix air into the water, can cut water consumption by 700 gallons per year.

75. Most water heaters come from the factory set at 140 degrees — hot enough to scald. Turn it down to 120 degrees to avoid a safety risk, save money, and slow mineral buildup and corrosion in your water heater and pipes.

76. The next time your water heater quits, replace it with a tankless heater that costs about the same but is likely to last more than 20 years, as opposed to the 10- to 15-year life expectancy of a tank heater. Plus, tankless models are 24 to 34 percent more energy efficient. But tankless heaters can heat only so much water at once, so if you like to shower and run several appliances at once or have a large household, you may need more than one.

77. Stop prewashing dishes if you have a modern dishwasher. It's not necessary. Just scrape them off thoroughly into the garbage and load them. You'll save about 55,000 gallons of water over the lifetime of the dishwasher. That can save about several hundreds of dollars, plus it's good for the environment — and avoids lots of unnecessary work.

78. Wash clothes in cold water. You'll save around $60 in energy costs a year. Plus it's gentler on your clothes and protects them from fading, shrinking, or bleeding. With today's detergents, your clothes will be just as clean.

79. Install a low-flow showerhead. You won't even notice the difference, because a low-flow fixture reduces the volume of water but does not affect the water pressure in any way. Save 2,900 gallons a year, according to the U.S. Environmental Protection Agency.

80. Insulate your hot water lines. Preformed foam insulation jackets slip over hot water pipes. You can easily lower your energy bill by $40 per year.

Zapping Your Electricity Bill

81. Keep your stovetop shiny. When the metal pans that surround burners on older stovetops become blackened from charred spillover, they absorb heat. When they are clean and shiny, they reflect heat and require less energy to cook food.

82. If the dish you are making will fit in your toaster oven, cook it in there. You can slash the energy cost by more than half over a full-size electric oven. You save time, too, because a toaster oven preheats much faster than a full-size oven.

83. Banish power vampires. The modern home has lots of devices that suck electricity even when turned off, costing an average of $100 per year, according to the U.S. Department of Energy. Chargers for phones, tablets, and other cordless devices drink juice even when they are not charging anything — so unplug them. Likewise, unplug televisions, computers, cable boxes, and game consoles — anything with a little indicator light.

84. Ask your utility companies for help. If you are having trouble paying your utility bill or want more information on how to lower your energy bills, your utility company should be your first contact. Many offer budget-billing programs in which you can pay a set amount each month.

Some offer special protections for customers who have disabilities, are on Supplemental Security Income, are on medical life-support equipment, or are having difficulty paying their bill. The utility company will devise an affordable payment plan or put you in touch with a nonprofit that may be able to help. Ask about rate options as well. Some offer a low-income rate discount. Others offer time-of-use rates that lower bills if you can move your consumption off-peak.

85. Install motion detectors. These sensors can be connected to lights, fans, or any other electrical device. They save energy dollars by automatically turning on the electrical device when you enter a room or area of your property and turning the device off when you leave. They can also make your home more secure by automatically turning on exterior lights if there is an intruder.

86. Upgrade to LED lighting. You can cut the amount of energy used by your light bulbs by up to 90 percent by switching to light-emitting diodes (LEDs) from traditional incandescent bulbs. LEDs also last 25 times longer, meaning you won't spend as much on new bulbs over time.

87. Test for a tight seal on your refrigerator by closing the door on a dollar bill; if you can easily pull the dollar out, the seal needs replacing.

88. Verify your fridge settings. Place a thermometer in your refrigerator overnight and check it in the morning: The ideal temperature for food safety is slightly below 40 degrees, according to the U.S. Food and Drug Administration. Too cold wastes energy and money. Too warm is unsafe. If the temperature is off, adjust accordingly.

89. Upgrade your appliances. Sure, that old refrigerator has been running since 1963. But it's probably sucking up a lot of juice while it's cooling your beer. New appliances with the Energy Star designation are more efficient than average appliances. Energy Star televisions, for example, use 3 watts or less when they are turned off, which is about 50 percent less than average.

The U.S. Environmental Protection Agency keeps a list of the most energy-efficient appliances at www.energystar.gov/products.

Lowering Heating and Cooling Costs

90. Lowering your home's temperature by 7 to 10 degrees for eight hours a day in the winter could save you up to 10 percent a year on your heating bill. To help regulate your household temperature, install a programmable thermostat so the settings change automatically.

91. Draw the blinds when the summer sun is blazing. About 76 percent of the sunlight that hits your windows enters to generate heat inside your home, according to the U.S. Department of Energy. A recent study found that 75 percent of blinds stay in the same position every day. Medium-colored draperies with white-plastic backings can reduce heat gains by 33 percent.

92. If you have a ceiling fan, use it. The U.S. Department of Energy says that when you use air conditioning, a ceiling fan will let you raise the thermostat about four degrees in the summer. Fans that carry the Energy Star label move air 20 percent more efficiently than those that don't. In the summer, you should set ceiling fans to go counterclockwise to blow air downward, according to Home Depot.

93. Inspect for leaks at windows and doors with a candle or lighted incense stick. Sealing them can cut a $1,000 heating and cooling bill by $200. Really! Gaps can reduce air-conditioning efficiency by 20 percent or more. Hold a candle or an incense stick to the seams where two ducts connect; the smoke will tell you whether air is escaping. Tape it!

94. Seal around outlets and switches. Stop chilly drafts by installing inexpensive foam gaskets available at most home improvement centers.

95. Staying cool is tough enough during a massive heat wave, but add soaring energy prices and inflation to the mix and it can be downright expensive, too. In 2022, energy costs were up 41.6 percent year over year.

Blasting the air conditioner all day and stocking up on an endless supply of bottled water aren't your only options. Here are other ways to stay cool without breaking the bank.

- **Give your air conditioner a tune-up.** If you do run your air conditioner, make sure it's operating as efficiently as possible. Otherwise, the unit has to work harder, which means more money spent on energy. Simple upkeep, like changing the filters, can improve the unit's performance. Experts say that with rising costs, you are trying to extend the lifetime of the unit so you don't have to replace it in the near term. If your air conditioner has an energy-saver mode, use it.

- **Shun the oven and dryer.** Reconsider cooking a three-course meal in a heat wave. Ovens give off heat, warming the room by a couple of degrees. The same goes for your dryer, which emits heat when in use. Avoiding it when the temperature is sizzling can be a cool strategy. Take advantage of the heat and air-dry your clothes.

- **Stay hydrated.** Drinking plenty of water and using ice will lower your body temperature, keeping your cooler. You may not need to pay for bottled water; look into the safety of your tap water.

- **Keep it light.** In cold weather wear a sweater, but in extreme heat the fewer clothes the better. Wearing loose-fitting, lightweight clothes and sleeping with sheets instead of heavy blankets can go a long way toward keeping you cool.

- **Tap your community.** Many communities across the country provide places for people to stay cool during the summer months, including community centers, cooling stations, malls, and libraries. They are usually air-conditioned and don't charge admission fees. Museums, movie theaters, and playhouses can be great places to stay cool and be entertained.

- **Shop around to save.** Stocking up on water (if you don't drink your tap water), ice cream, ices, or whatever you need to stay cool can add up. Without a doubt, inflation is making groceries more expensive, but take advantage of sales, loyalty clubs, and coupons. Pay attention to the price per unit when purchasing water. You want to ensure you're getting the most for your money. If possible, buy your water in bulk to save.

96. Get a furnace filter subscription. Changing your furnace filter every three months reduces heating bills and prolongs furnace life. But who remembers? Get a filter subscription (many online stores offer them) and stick in a new filter whenever one arrives.

97. Cover your windows. Homes lose about 30 percent of their heating energy through windows in the winter, and 76 percent of sunlight that falls on double-pane windows becomes heat in the summer. Consider blackout curtains.

98. Don't cover vents. Make sure your heating and cooling air vents aren't blocked by rugs, bookcases, or other furnishings. Blocking vents strains the furnace, shortening its life and increasing your energy bill.

99. Stop fireplace drafts. Dampers alone rarely stop the flow of air through your chimney; a reusable inflatable plug or chimney draft stopper helps seal out the cold.

100. Reinforce windows. If you have single-pane windows and can't afford to add outside storm windows, install custom-fit acrylic or glass panes instead. These interior storm windows can be pressed into place and sealed to create an airtight fit.

101. Reduce air-conditioning costs by as much as 10 percent by keeping AC condensers and window units shaded, perhaps by installing an overhead awning.

102. For whole house HVAC, inspect the ductwork carefully and seal any seams or gaps. Doing so reduces the amount of chilled or heated air escaping through the ductwork by up to 20 percent.

103. Many energy providers offer free or subsidized energy audits, which can identify problem areas in your home and offer suggestions and discounted solutions to fix them. They may also offer discounts for low-income users or deals for those who agree to preheat their home during off-peak hours.

104. Tap into energy assistance aid with the following programs:

- **Low-Income Home Energy Assistance Program (LIHEAP):** The Low-Income Home Energy Assistance Program, or LIHEAP, is a federal program that helps millions of low-income Americans afford to heat and cool their homes. If you need help paying your utility bills, replacing your furnace, weatherizing your home, or making other energy-related improvements, you can apply. Operated by the states, LIHEAP also provides crisis or emergency assistance for people who have received a shut-off notice or had their service disconnected.

  Details of the program vary by state. To apply, contact your state LIHEAP office or reach out through the National Energy Assistance Referral hotline at 866-674-6327.

- **Weatherization Assistance Program (WAP):** Weatherization is the best way to cut utility bills. The Weatherization Assistance Program, or WAP, helps low-income families lower their energy bills by making their homes more energy efficient. The U.S. Department of Energy provides funding to states, U.S. overseas territories, and Indian tribal governments. Those governments have a network of nonprofits, community groups, and local government agencies that provide weatherization services to households in each state. More information is available at www.energy.gov/eere/wap/weatherization-assistance-program or 888-771-9404. Special preference goes to families with someone 60 or older, children, or one or more members with a disability.

Tech to Save You Money

105. Get a smart thermostat. In addition to operating on a set schedule, smart thermostats learn your temperature preferences, and some can sense if someone is in the room. You can operate them from your smartphone, tablet, or laptop to make the house cozy when you return.

106. Buy a smart sprinkler controller. Tell the controller what type of soil, plants, or lawn you are watering, and the device will factor in the weather conditions and weather forecast to deliver exactly the amount of water your plants need.

Fixing Up Your Home on the Cheap

Did you know you can save hundreds of dollars when taking care of your home and yard? Whether you're cleaning, maintaining, decorating, or upgrading, there are always new and effective ways to trim costs and keep more of your cash in your pocket. Try some of these today!

Saving on Cleaning Supplies

107. Mix 8 ounces of water, 2 ounces of vinegar, and 2 pumps of dish detergent into a spray bottle. This low-cost solution cleans rug stains as well as most surfaces, including countertops, like magic. Of course, try it first on a small area to make sure it does not damage the material.

108. Make your own window cleaner. Put 2 cups water, ½ cup distilled vinegar, and 10 drops of any essential oil (lemon smells nice) in a spray bottle. Shake before using.

109. For a nontoxic oven cleaner, mix 2 cups baking soda and ¾ cup of water to create a spreadable paste. Scrape gunk off the sides and bottom of your oven with a wooden spatula, then spread the paste. Leave overnight; then clean with a sponge.

110. To remove carpet stains, spray a mixture of two-thirds warm water and one-third ammonia on the stain. Put an old towel over the stain and run a hot iron on the steam setting over the towel. The heat lifts the stain from the carpet into the towel. Spot-test first.

111. Slice your sponge budget in half. One study found that kitchen sponges generally are germier than toilets and are able to spread dangerous bacteria. Sanitizing or microwaving a sponge doesn't kill all germs, so it's best to replace them weekly. That's expensive, but you can cut your sponge costs with scissors.

Painting, Decorating, and Repairing Your Home

112. Find the same rich colors offered by high-end paint companies for less by taking their chips to a hardware store that can match the color.

113. Paint stores often sell gallons for a fraction of the price after they were custom mixed and the customer decided not to buy them.

114. Have an empty wall that's dying for some art? Go through your garage or storage to find interesting pieces of fabric or wallpaper and insert them into picture frames.

115. Use color strategically. Are your rooms painted different colors that don't flow together? Don't repaint. Instead, decorate one room with inexpensive pillows, vases, or throws in the color of the next room.

116. Swap hardware finishes. For under $10, Rub 'n Buff allows you to change the finish of faucets, metal knobs, and more. Or you can use Rust-Oleum spray paint in bronze, black, or gold to change the look — also under $10. Place the hardware on a large piece of cardboard and apply several coats.

117. Transform your kitchen for a few hundred bucks by replacing the faucet, changing door handles and pulls, and painting or even removing cabinet doors.

118. Instead of spending hundreds or even thousands of dollars on a new bathroom or kitchen countertop or backsplash, use broken pottery, glass, mirror, shells, and other interesting materials to create and install a fabulous mosaic — designed by you — for well under $100. Get some cement backer board from your local building materials store plus the materials for the mosaic, mortar, and grout.

119. Decorate with a mix of high and low and old and new, such as hand-me-down antiques and flea market vintage next to something new and inexpensive. The old pieces add soul to the room, which you can blend with Target or IKEA furniture.

120. Bring a little outdoors in. Transform old patio seating into a new piece for inside your home. Clean, spray-paint, and add a cushion and throw pillow for the final touches and — wow! — you have a new accent chair.

121. Give chairs a redo. Reupholstering worn and drab dining room or kitchen chairs can cost well over $100 each. Give them a modern makeover for less than $50 total with cloth shower curtains. Just remove seats from chair frames, measure, cut, and use a staple gun to attach the cloth.

122. Do it yourself and save big bucks. Tutorials online show you how to regrout a bathtub, upholster chairs, and more. For example, a video showing how to fix the latch spring on a microwave door could save the $150 to $300 you'd spend on a new appliance.

123. Get your stuff fixed for free. At Repair Café events nation-wide, volunteers help fix a variety of household items. Find one at repaircafe.org/en. You could save $100 by fixing that old lamp. Or visit www.needhelppayingbills.com/html/information_on_home_repair_pro.html to find other resources for help fixing things. You can also find free how-to guides, videos, and workshops to help make your home beautiful, safe, and comfortable at aarp.org/livable-communities.

124. Give your front entrance a makeover. "Painting your door with a pop of color — yellow, aubergine, orange, or black — can make your house the most stylish one on the block," says Ty Pennington, designer, carpenter, author, and host of HGTV's *Battle on the Beach*. The result is a look that's "modern, sophisticated, and clean." With just a gallon of paint, it's inexpensive, and the good news is, "If you hate it, you can repaint it."

125. With Porch Home Services, you get 5 percent off small jobs done by a Porch handyman and enhanced property protection for both small jobs and major home improvements. Plus, you get complimentary access to a dedicated Porch Home Assistant team to help book and manage your projects. Porch professionals can help with various home projects, landscaping, decorating, and more. Learn more at aarp.org/porch-home-services.

126. Spring isn't just a time for cleaning. It's also a perfect time to look at your living space with a critical eye — and to get creative. Your home may need refreshing with some simple and inexpensive DIY home improvement projects.

Try vintage and second-hand sources to get the most bang for your buck and acquire one-of-a-kind pieces.

Here are some ideas to refresh the interior or exterior of your home:

- **Create artwork.** Art adds color and personality to a room. One idea is to get your own photographs printed on canvas, metal, or wood. You also can buy inexpensive frames for artsy postcards or greeting cards you already have.

- **Install floor tiles.** Jazz up a small space, such as a laundry room, with vinyl peel-and-stick floor tiles in bold geometric designs. Faux wood makes a mudroom or bathroom feel cozier. The tiles are easy to install, clean, and replace.

- **Embrace outdoor living.** Create a new outdoor seating space by simply placing a bench on your front porch or making a patio from pea gravel and then adding comfy furniture.

- **Make a statement with bathroom mirrors.** Bathroom mirrors today are more than functional. Go modern with a round metal-framed mirror, retro with a starburst version, or rustic with a wood-framed mirror.

- **Add a kitchen backsplash.** Peel-and-stick ceramic or glass tile sheets make it easy to protect the wall behind your stove and above counters and modernize the look of your kitchen.

- **Upgrade lighting.** Indoor lighting can change the mood of a room. Add more lamps or choose lightbulbs based on their kelvin temperature — designated as "k" on packaging — which is a scientific measurement for the color of light. Replicate daylight around 4,000 kelvin for kitchens, offices, and bathrooms. Outdoors, add lights along pathways and driveways, which will also help to prevent falls.

- **Go green.** Beautify the front of your home or patio by planting flowers and greenery in large, decorative pots. Choose one large plant or several smaller plants in varying shades and heights. Indoors, plants add color and scent to a home. They're also good for your health: NASA research found that houseplants help purify the air of toxins by releasing oxygen and absorbing carbon dioxide.

- **Conceal clutter.** Many people have more stuff than they need. If you have yard equipment or sports gear without a home, consider building a fence to hide it. It's easier and less expensive than erecting a shed.

Finding Great Deals on Home Goods

127. Consider shopping at ReStore. Habitat for Humanity ReStore locations often have surplus building materials, appliances, and used furnishings that are offered at great prices at hundreds of ReStore locations in the United States. To find the closest one, check habitat.org/restores.

128. Discover architectural salvage shops. They offer a large, low-cost selection of gently used building materials, ranging from wood doors to plumbing fixtures. Vintage pieces add unmistakable flair to a home.

129. Barter your way to remodeling. Swap meets — where people trade decorative objects, building supplies, and labor — are growing in popularity and can be an inexpensive way to redecorate and remodel your home. Try SwapMadness.com or SwapMeetDirectory.com, or search "swap meet near me."

130. Know the retail seasons. January is the time to buy furniture and linens. April brings deals on gardening supplies and outdoor decor. May is the month to purchase mattresses. The best time to buy a grill is after Labor Day. Shop in October for appliances and November for cookware.

Landscaping for (Nearly) Free

131. Don't drench your lawn. It needs just 1 inch of water per week, including rain. Sprinklers often deliver much more than that. Put a coffee mug under the sprinkler and stick a ruler in it when you're done watering. If you've collected 2 inches of water, you are spending about $150 a month during the summer on wasted water.

132. Get a rain barrel. Connected to your home's storm gutters, it will collect water for later use on your lawn, vegetable garden, or car.

133. Watering and cutting make the grass in your yard the most expensive and labor-intensive part of the property. Americans spend about $29 billion annually on their lawns — that's about $90 per person. Be creative. Patios, decks, planting beds, and rock and gravel patches can add visual interest to your property while saving you money.

134. Get a free tree. Street tree and Arbor Day programs across the United States offer free trees to residents. Find one by searching "free trees" and the name of your state or community.

135. Mulch for free — or cheap. Many towns make massive amounts of mulch and offer it free to residents. Search online for your county name and "free mulch" to see if it (or free compost) is offered. Save a few dollars per 2 cubic feet of mulch or per cubic foot of compost.

Can't find free mulch? Use mulch alternatives. Reserve pricey bark mulch for the front of the flower bed. Use dried leaves you've chopped and bagged with your lawn mower in less visible spots. You can also put down cardboard and then cover it with an inch or two of mulch.

Another idea is to mulch with free wood chips. Check with your local tree care companies, utility companies, and your city. Used as mulch, wood chips not only suppress weeds but also provide nutrients that can reduce the need to buy fertilizer.

136. Trees, flowers, and other plants that are native to the region where you live will grow successfully with little or no watering, fertilizer, or other human attention once they are established. Use local plants and save money while increasing your summer hammock time. Check with a local county extension office or nursery to find out what native drought-resistant plants grow in your area.

137. Join a plant group on social media. Online gardening groups where members offer excess plants for free are thriving. Search social media platforms for local groups that offer useful, timely advice about plants tailored to your area.

138. Know your bulbs. Photograph your flowering bulbs in the spring so that in the fall you don't waste money by buying what you already have.

139. Save money on weed killers by spreading several layers of newspaper on the soil before mulching over them in the garden. This blocks weeds from growing and helps retain moisture, so you save even more by needing to water plants less.

You can avoid expensive and toxic weed killers by dousing weeds with scalding water left over after boiling potatoes or pasta.

Most weeds can also be killed with an inexpensive and eco-friendly spray made from 1 gallon of white distilled vinegar mixed with 1 ounce of liquid dish soap.

140. Get tools for less. On sites like Craigslist, Facebook Marketplace, and Freecycle.org, and apps like Letgo, Nextdoor, and OfferUp, you can dig up new or used supplies at low cost or maybe even for free. And search the internet to see whether there's a "tool library" in your area — either gratis or subscription based.

Shopping with Savvy

Whether you're shopping online or in brick-and-mortar stores, try using these simple tips to save on everything from toothpaste to furniture to electronics.

Saving with Discounts, Coupons, Gift Cards, and Cash Back

141. Consider signing up for texts from your favorite stores. Surprisingly, you often can get better discounts from a store's text message stream than from its emails. You can unsubscribe once you've made purchases.

142. Check for promo codes online before finalizing any purchase. Just search "promo code" or "discount code" and the name of the store or product.

143. Have your computer search for savings. Free browser extensions such as PayPal Honey, RetailMeNot Deal Finder, and Slickdeals can automatically find and apply coupon codes at checkout for you. These extensions work with multiple browsers. When you shop online, click on the icon and it searches for coupons.

One option for installing browser extensions on Chrome, Firefox, or Microsoft Edge is to visit the official store on the web and look at the list of available extensions.

- Read each description carefully, noting the number of downloads, ratings, and user comments. Pay special attention to the most recent version, because updates to a browser may make an extension work incorrectly.

- Click on the button of the extension you want, likely titled **Add to [name of browser]**.

- Scrutinize any alerts that pop up with some extensions if certain permissions or data are required. These can give you a second chance to consider how much of your browsing habits may be tracked.

Apple Safari requires you to download extensions in the browser, and other web browsers give you the same option. In Safari, do the following:

- Click the **Safari** pull-down menu at the top of your Mac screen to the right of the Apple symbol.

- Select **Safari Extensions. . .**, second from the top. This puts you in the Safari extensions area of the Apple App Store.

- Browse available extensions and accompanying descriptions, including lists such as Top Free Apps and Top Paid Apps.

- Click **Get** on the browser extension you seek.

To get to the extension stores for other browsers while you're using them, do this:

- For Chrome, go to **Window | Extensions**. The Chrome extensions you have now will display. Click on the hamburger menu icon ≡ | **Open Chrome Web Store**. A new tab will open.

- For Edge, click on the puzzle piece icon to the right of your browser's address bar, then **Open Microsoft Edge Add-ons**.

- For Firefox, look under **Tools | Add-ons and Themes**. You'll get some suggestions and a button to search for more.

You can then follow the preceding instructions to download extensions.

144. Earn shopping points for taking surveys, watching videos, or playing games at InboxDollars.com, SurveyJunkie.com, and Swagbucks.com. Redeem points for cash or gift cards at major retailers. You might save $5 on your next purchase.

145. Buy discounted gift cards. Many gift card recipients sell them at a discount on sites like CardCash.com, CardCookie.com, and Giftcards.com. That can mean bargains. You can also buy other people's unwanted gift cards at a discount through sites like GiftCardBin.com, GiftCardGranny.com, Raise.com, and many more.

146. AARP members and nonmembers can sign up for AARP's loyalty program, AARP Rewards (aarp.org/rewards), to earn points you can trade in for discounted gift cards and more. AARP members earn 50 percent more. AARP Rewards is free, and you earn points by completing fun and enriching activities on aarp.org/rewards.

147. When you go to an online retailer through a cash-back program like Ibotta (home.ibotta.com), Mr. Rebates (www.mrrebates.com), or Rakuten (www.rakuten.com), you'll get a credit returned to you as cash. The rebates are usually 1 to 5 percent but can be higher.

OLDER
ADULTS

148. Many retailers, including Kohl's, Ross Dress for Less, and Belk, offer discounts to older people, usually over 55, on certain days of the week or month. Some grocery stores and pharmacies do the same. Ask at your local store.

149. Get outlet deals. You no longer have to schlep to an outlet mall to get deals at factory stores. Instead, you can get outlet deals online from retailers like Chico's (chicosofftherack.com), J.Crew (factory.jcrew.com), and Zales (zalesoutlet.com). Simply do an online search for your favorite store and the word "outlet" to see whether it has online shopping.

Getting First-Rate Stuff Secondhand

150. Snag great stuff at secondhand shops. Donations are often local, so head for thrift stores in wealthier neighborhoods. Find stores at thethriftshopper.com or thriftstore listings.com, or search online for "secondhand stores" or "thrift stores near me." When you go, shop early in the week — many donations come in over the weekend. And watch for hidden bargains. Thrift stores often set prices by category, say, $3 per shirt, no matter what the brand.

151. Goodwill has an online auction site (shopgoodwill.com) where you can bid on treasures from Goodwill thrift stores across the country.

152. Scope out estate sales for jewelry, furnishings, or tools. You'll frequently find top-quality stuff, often just lightly used, and sometimes at super low prices. Many now also offer online auctions.

153. Yard sales in your area can be found at yardsalesearch.com and yardsaletreasuremap.com. The sites track sales then give you the when, where, and what you'll find. Don't be shy about getting there early to grab the best stuff.

154. Join a Buy Nothing Facebook group in your area or city to find freebies. Facebook's Buy Nothing Project aims to make decluttering and getting new items easy. Or check out your local Freecycle network (freecycle.org), which aims to encourage reuse to keep stuff out of landfills.

155. Buy reconditioned products. That means it's been returned to the factory where it was inspected and refurbished to working order. Ignore the scuff mark, but make sure it comes with a warranty. For example, a cordless drill that goes for $238 new can be bought refurbished for $157.

Buying Certain Items at Certain Times of the Year

156. Wait for the holidays for big purchases. Retailers (both online and brick-and-mortar) wait for three-day weekends, like Memorial Day or Labor Day, to offer their best deals on big-ticket items like appliances, mattresses, and furniture. That's also when many outlet centers sell a coupon book for about $5 that gives extra discounts, potentially worth hundreds.

157. Do a postseason stock-up shop. The best time to replace worn-out clothes, gear, or supplies is when their season has just ended. For example, a gas grill at one hardware store was listed at $299 during the summer and then marked down to $249 after the season. Savings: $50.

158. Keep an opportunity list. When something you wear or use frequently nears the end of its useful life, put it on a list of items to be replaced when the price is right. For example, replace sandals at summer's end. Besides saving money, they'll be on hand for the start of next summer.

159. Prime Day is Amazon Prime's biggest sale of the year, in the past held once over the summer and once in the fall, each for 48 hours. Not a member? Sign up for a free trial to take advantage of the savings and then cancel it once Prime Day has passed. If you're not sure whether a price is truly a deal, go to the CamelCamelCamel website, which will show you an item's price history on Amazon. Visit https://camelcamel camel.com/.

Saving Even More Money

160. Haggle chat! If a chat box pops up while you're shopping online, type in that you're interested in the item but it's a bit too costly. You may be offered a lower price.

161. Don't save your credit card information online. Retailers want it to be as easy as possible for you to check out, but adding a few steps to the process may make you less likely to give in to impulse purchases.

162. Shop beyond Amazon. Amazon is so easy to use that it can become a habit. Before you order, search online for the best price — including shipping — for the item you want to purchase. Smaller retailers as well as big-box online services from Costco, Target, and Walmart sometimes offer better deals. And online-only retailers like eBay, Newegg for electronics, and new ventures may be cheaper. Check ratings and the Better Business Bureau (www.bbb.org) if you're not familiar with the company.

163. Treat everything as returnable. Don't throw up your hands if a new purchase breaks or you decide you don't like it. Many merchants and manufacturers will give you a replacement for free, no questions asked, with or without a receipt — but you have to ask.

164. Don't rush to buy a protection plan. Many retailers offer extended warranties, but experts say they usually aren't worth it. Also, you may already have a free extended warranty through the credit card you use for the purchase.

165. Buy staples by subscription. Many online stores offer pet food, toilet paper, toothpaste, and more if you sign up to receive the product on a set schedule. You can save up to 15 percent, and you can easily change the schedule or cancel the service altogether.

166. Students can get half off the current Amazon membership pricing at www.amazon.com/joinstudent.

STUDENTS **167.** Whatever you're buying, check the prices of different color options. You could save a bundle — on clothes, earphones, yoga mats, athletic shoes, and more.

168. AARP members can get exclusive Walgreens cash rewards. When you link your AARP and myWalgreens memberships, you'll earn 10 percent Walgreens Cash rewards on Walgreens branded health and wellness products, 7 percent Walgreens Cash rewards on Walgreens branded beauty products, and 3 percent Walgreens Cash rewards on other eligible beauty purchases. For full details, visit aarp.org/walgreens-benefit.

Tech to Save You Money

169. Scan to find the lowest price using the Barcode Lookup Mobile or ShopSavvy app. We spotted a waffle maker at one store for $37.78. We scanned the bar code with ShopSavvy app and found it at a nearby store for $29.92.

170. Get retroactive refunds. Some stores will refund the difference if the price drops soon after you buy an item. The Earny and Sift apps find and claim price drops.

171. Earn cash back via cash-back apps such as BeFrugal, Ibotta, and Rakuten.

172. Find AARP member discounts for local stores using the AARP app or at memberoffers.aarp.org/shopping.

Being Clever about Clothes Shopping

How can you save money on your wardrobe while still looking stylish? Shopping smart. No matter your age, style, gender, or income, you'll look great with these secrets from our experts.

Shopping Strategically

173. Think 30 and three. Don't buy something unless you will wear it at least 30 times and it will go with at least three other items in your closet. Avoid "conditional" clothing — items that pair only with that one pair of slacks or shoes. You want all your clothing pieces to be interchangeable.

174. Take the care instructions printed on the label seriously regarding things like temperature for the wash water and how to dry. Materials improperly cared for will shrink, fade, or wear down over time. Check the label before you buy. Don't spend money on clothing you can't easily care for.

175. Put an end to costly trips to the dry cleaner. If you want to save on dry cleaning, avoid clothes labeled "dry clean only." You can often hand-wash silk, linen, wools, cashmere, and some synthetic blends that are labeled "dry clean."

Fill your sink with cold water and some mild detergent or shampoo and swish it around till sudsy. Do one item at a time, keeping whites, pales, brights, and darks separate. Dip a Q-tip in the water and do a colorfast test on a small, not too visible spot on the item. No dye transfers? You're okay. Let your item soak for 20 minutes. Drain, refill with cold water, and dip until no more suds appear.

Lay the item on a towel and roll it up to gently press out excess water (no squeezing or wringing!). Then unroll and move the item to a dry towel and reshape — do not hang. Allow plenty of time to air dry.

176. Create a color palette. Many people shop without considering a cohesive wardrobe palette, so they end up with items that rarely get worn. Pick about five colors you like the most and stick to them when shopping.

177. Shop your own closet. Organize clothes by category and color so you know exactly what you have. When you see five pairs of black pants hanging together, you (hopefully!) won't buy another.

178. Take advantage of petite feet. Fashionable girls' shoes and sandals are a fraction of the cost of adult shoes. Same holds true for sneakers. For example, Air Jordan 1, Chuck Taylor Converse, and Nike Air Force 1 for big kids cost far less than the same style for adults.

179. Some department and clothing stores offer discounts for older adults. Kohl's, for instance, offers a 15 percent discount every Wednesday for customers 60+. Ross Dress for Less offers 10 percent off on Tuesdays for people 55+. Not all chains apply discounts nationally. Ask for senior discounts at stores you frequent.

OLDER ADULTS

180. Know when to shop. Buy season-ending store clearance clothing for next year. You can frequently save up to 90 percent on after-season sales, so sweaters, suits, and coats in January; shorts and swimsuits in July. Other good times to buy: workout clothes and lingerie in June, denim in October, and sneakers in November.

181. Never search for another lost sock again. Buy one brand in one color, so all your socks match. When you lose a sock or wear a hole in it, keep the other as a spare.

MILITARY & VETERANS

182. If you are a veteran, an active service member, or a member of a military family, you are eligible for a variety of deals year-round from these nationally recognized apparel stores. *Tip:* Even if you don't see your favorite retailers listed here, they may offer military or veterans discounts. Some may be franchises of national chains that offer price cuts locally but not as part of an across-the-board program.

Note: Some require SheerID, a verification platform to confirm your eligibility with authoritative data sources, like the U.S. Department of Defense. Visit www.sheerid.com/privacy_overview/.

- **Adidas:** Military members can enjoy 30 percent off online and in stores, and 20 percent off at factory outlet stores. Visit www.adidas.com/us/discount-programs.

- **Allen Edmonds:** Veterans and active military members receive 15 percent off at the shoe retailer after verification through ID.me. Visit www.allenedmonds.com/about/exclusive-offers.

- **Ariat:** All active military members and veterans get a 10 percent discount after verifying their eligibility. Visit www.ariat.com/military-discount.

- **Asics:** A 40 percent discount on eligible online purchases is available to service members who verify their status with SheerID. Visit www.asics.com/us/en-us/discount-programs.html.

- **Bonobos:** Current and former military personnel are eligible for a 20 percent discount. Visit bonobos-military.sheerid.com/.

- **Buckle:** Active-duty military, veterans, spouses, and their dependents may receive a 10 percent discount on all merchandise after verifying their status with SheerID. Visit www.buckle.com/military.

- **Champion:** Military members, veterans, and their families can take advantage of a 10 percent discount through ID.me. Visit www.champion.com/military-id.

- **Cole Haan:** Active-duty military and veterans get 20 percent off after registering on the store's website. Visit www.colehaan.com/military.html.

- **Columbia:** Military members save 10 percent on their online purchases after verifying their status with ID.me. Visit hosted-pages.id.me/columbia-military.

- **Converse:** Active-duty military and their spouses and dependents get 10 percent off, as do reservists and veteran military personnel. Visit www.converse.com/c/military-discount.

- **Dockers:** All military members receive a 25 percent discount on Dockers apparel. Visit us.dockers.com/pages/military-discounts.

- **Eddie Bauer:** Military members, veterans, and their families receive a 10 percent discount. Visit www.eddiebauer.com/service/help?a=In-Store-Military-and-Educators-Discount---id--iaFfzaijRKekiojID59AHA.

- **Foot Locker:** Active-duty members, veterans, and their dependents save 10 percent on most purchases with Sheer ID verification. Visit help.footlocker.com/hc/en-us/categories/360002167454-Military-Discount.

- **Hanes:** All members of the military community receive 10 percent off at Hanes.com. Visit www.hanes.com/military-id.

- **Helly Hansen:** Active-duty military and veterans receive a 35 percent discount on online purchases. Visit www.hellyhansen.com/en_us/military.

- **Jansport:** Military members, veterans, and their dependents can unlock 30 percent off after verifying their eligibility. Visit www.jansport.com/sheerid/discount-for-military-medical-and-first-responders.html.

- **J.Crew Factory:** Anyone who has served or is currently serving in the armed forces and their registered dependents are eligible for a 15 percent discount on their purchases. Visit factory.jcrew.com/s/military-medical-first-responder-discount.

- **Kohl's:** Active-duty military, veterans, and their families are eligible for a 15 percent-off coupon for use in stores on Mondays. Visit cs.kohls.com/app/answers/detail/a_id/2926/~/servicemember-%28military%29-discount.

- **Levi's:** Military service members get a 15 percent discount on all Levi's apparel. Visit www.levi.com/US/en_US/features/military-discounts.

- **L.L.Bean:** Members of the armed forces and veterans may take 10 percent off their order. Visit www.llbean.com/llb/shop/517432?page=military-discount.

- **Lululemon:** Service members and military spouses receive 15 percent off through SheerID. Visit shop.lululemon.com/story/military-first-responder.

- **Manscaped:** Active-duty service members, veterans, and surviving spouses get 20 percent off and free shipping when verified through ID.me. Visit www.manscaped.com/pages/military-discounts.

- **Nike:** A 10 percent discount is provided to active-duty service members, veterans, and their families with SheerID. Visit www.nike.com/help/a/military-discount?.

- **The North Face:** Service members, veterans, and spouses and dependents of active-duty military receive a 10 percent discount. Visit www.thenorthface.com/en-us/help/the-north-face-military-discount-program.

- **Rack Room Shoes:** Military personnel and their families get 10 percent off any in-store purchase on Tuesdays and a 20 percent discount every Memorial Day, Fourth of July, and Veterans Day with valid military ID. Visit www.rackroomshoes.com/military-discount.

- **Reebok:** Military members get 50 percent off online orders. Select exclusions apply. Visit www.reebok.com/us/discount-programs.

- **Steve Madden:** Active and retired service members of the armed forces receive a 25 percent discount after verifying eligibility and receiving a promo code. Visit www.stevemadden.com/pages/military-discount?.

- **Sunglass Hut:** Active-duty service members, veterans, and military spouses and family members may take advantage of a 15 percent discount after verification through ID.me. Certain exclusions apply. Visit www.sunglasshut.com/us/sunglasses/special-offers?cid=PM-ACJ_190701-4484837_Siteplug_11489265&cjevent=ad32ce67128e11ed83e2b9920a82b838&cjdata=MXxOfDB8WXww.

- **Timberland:** Military members, registered spouses, and their dependents can save 10 percent on select items once service has been verified. Visit www.timberland.com/military-discount.html.

- **Under Armour:** Active-duty military members, veterans, and military spouses and family members save 20 percent on all purchases online and in stores. A 10 percent discount is applied at Under Armour factory stores. Visit www.underarmour.com/en-us/t/troop-id-instructions.html.

- **Vera Bradley:** A 15 percent discount is available for active-duty military, reservists, retirees, veterans, and military spouses and immediate family members who verify eligibility through ID.me. Visit verabradley.com/pages/appreciation-discount.

- **Vineyard Vines:** Active-duty military and veterans get 15 percent off almost all merchandise. Visit www.vineyardvines.com/verification-military/.

- **Yeti:** Discounts are offered to current service members and veterans on select products after verification through ID.me. Visit www.yeti.com/id-me.html.

Shopping Secondhand

183. RehashClothes.com has more than 10,000 items of clothing and accessories that its members can swap for just the cost of postage. See something you like? Offer a piece of clothing in exchange.

184. An average American discards 81 pounds of clothes every year. Some 66 percent ends up in landfills, and another 19 percent is incinerated, according to the U.S. Environmental Protection Agency.

So before you trash clothes you've outgrown or just grown tired of, consider a local clothing swap. Reach out to friends and neighbors and let the fun begin! Invite about 10 to 15 people of various sizes and shapes, host them indoors or outdoors, and have a few mirrors available.

185. At RentTheRunway.com and StyleLend.com, you can rent designer-label clothing, including formal wedding attire, at a fraction of the retail price.

186. Shop thrift stores virtually. Thrifters have a new way to find secondhand bargains and deals: online, through sites such as GoodwillFinds.com, Poshmark, Swap, TheRealReal, ThredUp, and Tradesy.

Sales in the secondhand and resale market are forecast to hit $54 billion in 2023. By 2026, they're expected to reach $82 billion, according to ThredUp.

Demand is driven by record-high inflation forcing consumers to seek bargains wherever they can find them.

The bargains can be huge if you don't mind purchasing used. But finding diamonds in the rough can prove more difficult online, where you can't try on the items you're shopping for and inspect them for damage as you would at your local thrift store.

It's not impossible. To help you navigate online thrifting, consider these seven strategies.

- **Select your site.** Whether you're shopping for vintage, luxury, or ripped blue jeans, there is a secondhand site for that. To save time, narrow your options to thrift sites that cater to what you are looking for. For instance, ThredUp and Vestiaire Collective are among those that specialize in selling designer and vintage apparel, while GoodwillFinds.com and Swap offer more general treasure hunting.

- **Have an open mind.** Shopping for a specific item on thrift sites can quickly become frustrating, which is why experts say to be broad-minded when looking for deals. Think of it the same way you would if you visited a brick-and-mortar thrift store: as a treasure hunt.

- **Know your size.** Many online thrift stores don't offer returns, and when they do, you're often required to pay for shipping. To avoid any purchasing blunders, it's important to know your size and the sizes of your family. Even better, take everyone's measurements. Many secondhand websites provide measurement details for each item they sell. That's a foolproof way to get the right fit. You can also stick to brands you're familiar with. That takes a lot of the sizing guesswork out of the equation.

- **Pay attention to details.** Most online thrift stores vet the products they sell to ensure they are not too damaged and are what they claim to be. The condition of the item is usually listed alongside photos. If there are multiple images, make sure to go through each one to spot any damage not listed in the product details.

- **Narrow your search with shopping tools.** One of the joys of online shopping is that you can sift through thousands of items at breakneck speed, thanks to filtering tools. Found on most secondhand sites, they let you browse based on size, product type, color, and other categories. Say you are on the hunt for a black shirt, size small. You can put that into the filter, and the website will show the items matching those criteria. Swap has a feature called "shop this style": You click on an outfit, and it kicks back every matching or similar product. GoodwillFinds.com has curated collections that make shopping easier, be it for Halloween costumes, fall sweaters, or home decor.

- **Consider signing up for emails.** Aim to save even more? Sign up for emails and alerts with your favorite internet thrift stores. Most of the secondhand sites let you do this and will send you deals and discounts from time to time. Some will give you a percentage off your first purchase and/or free shipping. If you're worried about your inbox getting flooded with thrift store emails, create a free email account to handle the influx of bargains.

- **Don't give up.** If you can't find what you are looking for, come back often. The websites update their inventory regularly, and what may have been hard to locate last week could be abundant the next. The key is to keep at it to get the best deals on items you want.

Tech to Save You Money

187. Tell the free Karma website (www.karmanow.com/) and mobile app what clothing, shoes, or accessories you are in the market for. Karma is linked to over 100,000 online stores worldwide and can tell you when there are sales, when stock of an item is low, or when it's available again.

188. ShopStyle (www.shopstyle.com), Google (https://shopping.google.com), and Bing (www.bing.com/shop) are search engines and mobile apps that filter the web for the best prices on whatever you need.

Saving on Hair, Beauty, and Personal Care

You don't need to spend top dollar for haircuts or health and beauty products. Check out these tips from our experts.

Cutting Costs on Hair and Massage Services

189. Save on haircuts by signing up to be a hair model at salonapprentice.com, where aspiring stylists practice their craft.

190. Try a beauty-school haircut. Search online for "beauty-school near me." Aveda Institute, Empire Beauty Schools, and Paul Mitchell Schools, for example, offer haircuts for under $15, sometimes with a shampoo or blow dry. That's much less than the usual cost of a woman's haircut at a salon.

191. Stretch your color. Make it a habit to stock up on chic, wide hairbands (your roots' new best friend), and get handy using a temporary touch-up — like Clairol Nice 'n Easy Touch Up, Color Wow Root Cover Up, dpHUE Color Touch-Up Spray, or L'Oréal Paris Magic Root Cover Up, where you can find standard and hard-to-find shades like strawberry blonde and auburn.

192. You'll pay less for massages and other spa services if you go to a beauty or massage school where students are getting hands-on experience for certification. Compared to a typical massage, these schools can charge half the price that graduates charge.

193. Enjoy a DIY facial massage. If you've ever had a facial at a spa or day spa, you know that how the aesthetician applies creams and masks is as important as the products themselves. Massaging on your creams and serums mindfully can stimulate circulation, help reduce puffiness under eyes and jaw, smooth expression lines, and erase tension.

Start by applying a skin serum or face oil for the necessary "slip." Use a low-cost jade roller or your fingers and gentle pressure in slow sweeping movements to massage from the center of your face outward, including your forehead and under-eye area. Then massage upward from neck to jawline to hairline and repeat the procedure. If you use a roller, store it in the fridge because the chilled stone helps deflate puffiness. You never want to work in a downward or inward movement, which only encourages gravity and expression lines.

Spending Less on Hair and Beauty Products

194. High-end cosmetic companies also make affordable brands, so you can save money without sacrificing quality. For example: Instead of Giorgio Armani Beauty, try Essie and Maybelline. All three brands are made by L'Oréal Paris. Estée Lauder produces MAC and Flirt Cosmetics. And the company that makes ultra-pricey La Prairie also sells Nivea and Eucerin.

195. Try starter kits. Twice a year, in January and then in May or June, many manufacturers offer skin care "starter kits" for as little as $30. They contain a useful, frugal mix of products in "deluxe trial-size" containers (usually about half the regular size). Spring versions usually include a sunscreen.

196. Use baby oil to remove eye makeup. At 25 cents an ounce, it works as well as many brand-name removers, which can cost several dollars an ounce.

197. Most commercial shampoos are concentrated and may dry out hair if used at full strength. Try diluting with 50 percent water and save up to $15 per bottle.

198. Don't buy salon hair products for everyday use. A brand-name conditioner may be around $25 for about 10 ounces. But a store-brand conditioner found at a national chain works well too at only a few dollars for roughly the same size.

199. Join a shave club. Pay about $2 for a razor cartridge at an online shave club like the Athena Club, Dollar Shave Club, or Harry's. Save a few bucks per cartridge compared with brand-name choices bought in a store.

200. Ladies, use men's shaving gel. It's usually cheaper. (That holds true for many grooming products packaged differently for men and women.)

201. Don't throw out beauty products that didn't work. If a face moisturizer or cleanser irritates your face, try it on your hands or pass it to a friend or relative. Use that facial oil on cuticles. Salvage an unflattering lipstick shade by mixing with plain lip balm to sheer the color and texture down to a wearable tint.

202. Whoever said nothing in life is free hasn't taken advantage of what you can get in the mail without paying a penny. In some instances, you have to be a brand ambassador; in other cases, you're required to provide personal information, fill out lengthy surveys, and/or test products. But if you're willing to give up some of your time and privacy, freebies by mail abound.

With that in mind, here's how to snag them and what you'll have to give up in return.

- **Razors:** There are several ways consumers can get razors and/or blades for free. The easiest is to sign up for email alerts and promotions from your favorite razor manufacturers. Bic,

Gillette, Philips, and Schick run promotions from time to time that include free razors and blades, which you won't know about unless you're a registered customer. You can also track your favorite brands on social media to find out about freebies that will come in the mail.

The razor companies aim to please and seek feedback from consumers when developing new products and services. They run focus groups and conduct surveys online, in person, and over the phone. Through these programs you not only test products but get to keep them. To take part, you sign up online and complete a survey, and the company will mail you products to test that fit your profile. With the Philips product tester program, you have to provide feedback and submit a review to keep the product.

If you're loyal to one brand and sign up for a subscription, you'll often receive a free razor and blades. With Gillette's program you get a free razor kit. All you're on tap for is $4 in shipping.

What you give up: Most of the time you're giving up your name, address, and email. If you become a product tester, the company may ask you more in-depth questions about your likes and dislikes and shopping habits.

- **Beauty items:** Focus groups are common in the beauty industry, with companies testing all manner of cosmetics and perfume. They seek a constant stream of feedback and rely on third parties to gather that for them. That's where survey companies such as BzzAgent (bzzagent.com) and PinkPanel (pinkpanel.com) come in. They find beauty enthusiasts to take surveys, review samples, and test products. In return they get to keep the products and, in some cases, get paid.

  What you give up: To join you have to fill out an application online. In addition to providing identifying information including your name, address, and email, you may have to answer a series of questions about your beauty habits. Check the privacy policy. Opt out of letting companies sell or share your personal information.

Making Your Own Health and Beauty Supplies

203. For mouthwash, put six sage leaves in a bottle. Dissolve 1 teaspoon Himalayan salt or Celtic sea salt in 5 ounces of boiling water and pour over the leaves and steep. Use daily after brushing teeth.

204. For bath oil, add a few drops of your favorite perfume or cologne to ¼ cup of baby oil, shake it up in a small jar, and add it to your bath.

205. Combine a cup of sugar and some olive oil to make an instant and effective body and foot exfoliant.

206. Remove nail polish stains with a homemade whitening paste. Mix one tablespoon hydrogen peroxide with two tablespoons baking soda and apply to polish-free nails — under tips, too — for 10 minutes. Wipe off residue. Then use a nail buffer to give nails a healthy, pinkish sheen.

207. Give yourself a facial on the cheap. Place cooled tea bags on puffy, red eyes to deflate and refresh (the combo of caffeine and tannin does it). Whisk two egg whites and apply as a facial mask for 20 minutes to tighten saggy skin, or mash a ripe avocado and apply to soothe dry skin.

Tech to Save You Money

208. Find AARP member discounts for local salons and spas on the AARP Now app or at memberoffers.aarp.org/shopping.

Getting Quality Healthcare (Including Insurance) for Less

Whether it's small acts or big lifestyle changes, you could save thousands of dollars in healthcare costs by taking action today. Here's to your health — and healthy cost savings!

Saving on Healthcare and Insurance

209. Read your bills carefully. Eight out of ten medical bills contain errors, so check to be sure you're not being overcharged. Always ask for itemized bills. If you have lots of bills, another option is to call in a medical bill negotiator to review your bills for errors and overcharges, and potentially save thousands of dollars.

210. Stay in your plan's network. Most health insurance plans offer in-network and out-of-network coverage. If you stay within the network of providers your plan offers, you can save big on out-of-pocket expenses.

211. Review your health insurance coverage every year. Your coverage may change from one year to the next, so it's important to review it during your open enrollment period. Changes can affect your monthly premiums, copays, deductibles, the services covered by your insurance, and the list of doctors who participate in the insurer's network. Avoid costly surprises come January 1.

212. Need surgery? Research cost-cutting alternatives to hospitals, such as outpatient facilities. The fees for a doctor and anesthesiologist may be similar, but typically, outpatient centers charge a fraction of the fee that hospitals charge.

213. Several weeks before a procedure, call your insurer and provider to confirm the procedure and providers involved in your care — such as a physician and anesthesiologist — are in your network and covered by your plan. If they're not all in-network, consider using another provider.

214. Enroll in a flexible spending account at work and pay thousands of dollars of out-of-pocket health bills with pretax dollars. Expenses such as premiums, copays, deductibles, dental work, and eyeglasses qualify. Check with the Internal Revenue Service for qualifying expenses. Plan carefully, though. FSAs have a use-it-or-lose-it penalty, meaning if you contribute more than you use, you forfeit the excess contribution.

215. Negotiate hospital bills even if you have insurance. Hospitals will often offer a discounted rate, especially if you pay cash. If you haven't met your deductible, the discounted price may cost you less than you'd pay out of pocket with insurance.

Contact the billing department at the hospital or medical practice to get the process started.

- **Get the data.** Figure out how much you can afford to pay, then look up the average cost for the procedure or treatment you underwent. Consider checking Healthcare Bluebook (www. healthcarebluebook.com/explore–home/) or FAIR Health Consumer (www.fairhealthconsumer.org/), websites where you can check typical prices in your area for a procedure or course of treatment.

If you're on Medicare, take a look, too, at what it pays for a procedure and the rate your health plan pays for the service at in-network facilities (visit www.medicare.gov/procedure-price-lookup/). If you were balance billed because out-of-network providers took part in your treatment without your knowledge (and charged you the balance between their fee and what insurance covered), these figures can serve as starting points for negotiation.

- **Consider "prompt pay."** Sometimes a medical provider will accept far less money if you agree to pay immediately. A doctor may rather work to reach a settlement than get nothing.

  If it's late in the year, you may have a better chance of striking a deal, some experts say, because hospitals, doctors, and other providers may be more open to negotiation when their financial offices are trying to close out the annual books.

- **Ask for an installment plan.** If you can't negotiate the bill down, ask the provider whether you can set up an interest-free payment schedule. It's important to know going in what you can afford to pay monthly and for how long. If you make your initial payments in full and on time, the billing office may be willing to reconsider a discount or write-off on the rest of the bill.

- **Get professional help.** When your bill is very high or you've exhausted your ability to negotiate on your own, think about hiring a professional, such as a medical billing advocate or an attorney who specializes in medical billing disputes. You can ask your state's bar association for a referral. (Visit www.findlaw.com/hirealawyer/choosing-the-right-lawyer/state-bar-associations.html.)

  Medical billing advocates work with patients to review bills for errors and negotiate lower costs. There are both for-profit and nonprofit advocates. The Patient Advocate Foundation, for example, will do this work for free, but only if you have a chronic, life-threatening, or debilitating medical condition that has been diagnosed.

Professional advocates either charge an hourly fee or take a percentage of what they save you.

In looking for a billing advocate, focus on the person's level of expertise. Many previously worked at insurance companies or in the billing offices at hospitals or medical practices; their websites should comprehensively list their skills, experience, and credentials. You can search for billing advocates in the online directories of industry groups such as the National Association of Healthcare Advocacy (www.nahac.com/), the Alliance of Professional Health Advocates (aphadvocates.org/), and the Alliance of Claims Assistance Professionals (claims.org/).

216. Get help in disputes. You have appeal rights when your insurance company denies a medical claim or pays less than you think it should. Most states have a consumer assistance program that can help you file appeals and resolve disputes.

MILITARY &
VETERANS

217. The Department of Veteran Affairs (VA) Caregiver Support Program offers clinical services to caregivers of eligible and covered veterans enrolled in the VA healthcare system. The program's mission is to promote the health and well-being of family caregivers who care for our nation's veterans, through education, resources, support, and services. Find details at www.caregiver.va.gov, or call 855-260-3274 toll-free.

Maximizing Your Medicare Benefits

218. **Sign up for Medicare at the right time.** If you are nearing Medicare eligibility, you have a window to sign up. If you miss this window, your monthly Medicare premiums may be higher. For help from AARP on your Medicare questions, check out AARP's *Medicare For Dummies* (published by Wiley).

219. Take advantage of the free services Medicare offers, such as many preventive tests and screenings. Be sure you meet the conditions for free services: You must go to a doctor who accepts the Medicare-approved cost as full payment, and you must observe any time limits for the test, such as once a year.

Free Medicare services include your annual wellness visit. This appointment gives you time with your doctor to look at long-term health needs and goals. Research shows that people who have them are more likely to get recommended influenza, pneumonia, and shingles vaccines, to receive recommended colon- and breast-cancer screenings, and to get a cholesterol check.

Keep in mind that a "wellness" visit by any other name would not be free. You can have a free "wellness" doctor visit once a year covered by Medicare, if you ask for it by that name. But if you ask for a "physical" — a more comprehensive exam — you'll be charged full price.

220. Check with Medicare before buying health equipment. The federal health insurance program will often pay part of the cost for walkers, canes, wheelchairs, and hospital beds.

221. Shop every year for a new Medicare plan. Open enrollment runs from October 1 through December 7. Prices and providers change often, so compare plans and change your enrollment at medicare.gov.

222. See if you qualify for the Medicare Savings Programs, federally funded programs administered by states, to help pay Medicare Part A and B premiums. Find out more at www.medicare.gov/medicare-savings-programs.

Cutting Your Prescription Costs

223. Check your drugs. Put all your medications — prescription, over-the-counter, even supplements and vitamins — into a bag and take them to your doctor's appointments. Ask whether you need them all. Many people are overprescribed, especially if they see several doctors for different medical issues. Having your meds reviewed periodically is also good for your health.

224. Consider generics. Authorized generics are made by the manufacturer of the brand-name version and have the same active and inactive ingredients. Thousands are on the market, including epinephrine pens and hepatitis C treatments. Insurance coverage varies, so check first.

225. Get a free prescription discount card through AARP Prescription Discounts provided by the OptumRx program. The card can be used to save on all FDA-approved medications at 66,000-plus participating retail pharmacies such as CVS Pharmacy, Walgreens Pharmacy, and Walmart Pharmacy. Visit aarp.org/rx-discounts.

226. Ask your pharmacist about the best deal. Congress banned pharmacist "gag clauses" — which prohibited pharmacists from voluntarily informing patients that their prescription medication may cost less if paid for directly instead of through insurance. That just means you have to ask; pharmacists aren't required to offer information about the best price without being asked.

227. Use a pharmacy discount card. A growing number of insurers, pharmacies, and other companies offer pharmacy discount cards that may get you as much as 80 percent off the list price of prescription drugs — making them more affordable if you don't have drug coverage or if your copay, coinsurance, or other insurance-backed cost is too high. Shop around online to find the best deal on the drugs you take.

228. Some supermarket and discount chains offer common medications for free. If your deductible is $10, for example, you'll save $120 a year on just one 30-day prescription. Ask the pharmacy department at your local stores which medications, if any, they offer for free. Often, you only need a doctor's prescription to qualify.

229. Got a long-term condition that requires prescription meds? Ask for a 90-day supply, and make a single copay every three months instead of one every 30 days.

230. Use patient assistance programs. Many of these pharmaceutical and medical device company-funded programs expanded during the pandemic. Check needymeds.org/pap for a list of current programs.

231. Take your medications regularly. It's important to take your medications exactly as prescribed. You can avoid costly hospital visits that often result from skipped doses.

232. Get help on drug costs. Medicare beneficiaries may qualify for the Extra Help program to cover prescriptions. You can potentially save thousands of dollars a year. Apply at socialsecurity.gov/extrahelp or call 800-772-1213.

233. Go to the Partnership for Prescription Assistance at https://medicineassistancetool.org/. Patients who qualify can save hundreds of dollars.

234. Prices vary significantly from pharmacy to pharmacy. To save up to 80 percent, try RxSaver or GoodRx — either the app or the website — that lets you search prescriptions, find prices near you, and get coupons to present at the pharmacy.

235. If you're taking a brand-name drug regularly, check the drugmaker's website to see whether it offers a coupon or discount card that can save you money.

236. For some meds, skip your insurance. Ask your pharmacist about the retail price of your prescription medication; it may be cheaper to pay that price.

237. If you're a Medicare recipient, shop every year for your Medicare Part D plan, too. Note that your expenses can be a lot lower if you buy prescription drugs from a pharmacy that your Part D plan calls "preferred" — meaning the pharmacy has agreed to charge reduced copays. Call your plan for preferred pharmacies in your area.

Taking Care of Your Teeth

238. No dental insurance? Dental practice membership plans may give you a set number of cleanings, exams, and X-rays for a discounted annual fee, plus a discount on fillings and other services. You can save $100 a year or more over the price of routine care. Your dentist may also be more inclined to negotiate more expensive procedures.

239. Talk to your dentist about X-rays. If you aren't at higher-than-normal risk for cavities, you may need dental X-rays only every two to three years, says the American Dental Association.

240. Invest in prevention. An in-office fluoride varnish or home treatment with a prescription toothpaste can repair eroded tooth enamel and stop early tooth decay from becoming a full-fledged cavity, which can save you money on a filling.

OLDER ADULTS

241. Find out whether you qualify for free dental care at `dental lifeline.org/our-state-programs/#DDS`. Donated Dental Services provides older adults with free comprehensive dental treatment. It operates through a volunteer network of more than 15,000 dentists and 3,400 dental labs across the United States.

242. Visit a community health clinic that offers reduced-cost or free dental care to people with low incomes. Visit `https://findhealthcenter.hrsa.gov/` to find a center near you and check to see whether it offers dental care. There may be a wait list, so apply early.

Looking for Savings on Eye Care and Glasses

243. Understand the features available for eyeglasses, and whether they're worth the extra cost.

- **High-index lenses:** Thinner, lighter, and more comfortable than regular lenses, they're a great choice for those with strong prescriptions — helping you avoid the "Coke bottle" look.

- **Polycarbonate lenses:** A type of high-index lens, they are highly durable (up to 10 times more impact resistant than average plastic), are scratch resistant, and have built-in UV protection.

- **Photochromic lenses:** These lenses react to ultraviolet (UV) light, staying clear indoors and darkening in sunlight. This is an economical add-on, good for those who don't want to carry around a pair of prescription sunglasses — with the caveat that they won't darken inside cars because windshields filter out the UV rays that trigger the color change. They also can be a smart choice for older patients, who may be beginning to get cataracts and need to protect their eyes from UV light. Different brands have different levels of darkness and reaction times, so take time to comparison shop.

- **Progressive lenses:** Doing bifocals one better, these lenses offer three prescriptions in one lens — up close and at a distance, with an intermediate distance (say, for computer viewing) in the center — allowing you to see all distances. They gradually change from each prescription, as you move your eyes down and up. This makes them a nice option for those who want only one pair of full-time glasses. They don't have that line across the lens you'll get with bifocals. Some people, though, have difficulty adjusting to them, including going up and down stairs.

- **High-definition (digital) lenses:** These lenses are to your eyes what high-definition (HD) technology is to TV. Based on a digital scan of your eyes, digital lenses can give you even crisper, clearer vision than conventional lenses. Take note: They generally cost up to 25 to 30 percent more than conventional glasses of the same material and design, and may only offer a slightly better view.

- **Anti-glare coating:** This add-on, often bundled with high-index and HD lenses, eliminates reflections from the surfaces of your lenses. That means more light is able to get through, enhancing the quality of your vision by doing away with annoying distractions — such as glare and halos many people see when driving at night. It also improves the look of your glasses: By reducing the glare bouncing off the surface of your lenses, they look practically invisible. On the downside, the anti-glare coating can get scratched or, over time, begin to peel off.

OLDER ADULTS

244. Get free eye care. People over 65 may be eligible for a free eye exam and care through the American Academy of Ophthalmology's EyeCare America program. Find out more at aao.org.

245. Frames, which can range from a few bucks to hundreds or even thousands of dollars, can be a big part of your total cost. Whether you're looking for standard plastic or pricey titanium wire frames, it pays to comparison shop. And when it comes to designer frames, you'll shell out more, but that doesn't mean the product is better. They may be made on the same assembly line, according to one expert.

- **Online retailers:** Companies like EyeBuyDirect, GlassesUSA, Warby Parker, and Zenni Optical have been giving the brick-and-mortar stores a run for their money — especially during the pandemic, when many people would rather shop from home. Many online stores have virtual try-on tools to help you get a good fit. (Warby Parker even allows you to try on five pairs at home, for free.) You can find a huge selection of well-made eyewear for under $150, though adding extras such as impact-resistant lenses with antireflective coating will drive up the price.

  Online retailers can also be a good way to nab discount designer frames as well as inexpensive ones (a search on Zenni uncovered a $6.95 pair of basic prescription rectangular glasses with anti-scratch coating and UV protection).

  If you're going to be wearing your glasses full time, it may pay to get professionally fitted. Check the return policy, in case you're not satisfied. Some online retailers offer no-questions-asked returns; others may offer another pair instead. And, if you have vision insurance, be sure the website accepts it (not all do).

  To buy online, you need a valid prescription and your pupillary distance (PD) measurement, which is the distance in millimeters between your pupils or from your pupils to the center of your nose bridge. This indicates where the company filling your prescription needs to place the optical center (or "sweet spot") of vision in the lenses, so you can see clearly. Many online retailers offer ways to determine your PD, including virtual eye exams. Apps may be able to do it, or you can ask your eye doctor to include it as part of an eye exam. Online suppliers typically place the spot in the geometric center of the lens, but sometimes the spot doesn't match your line of sight, and your vision will be affected.

- **Chain retailers and independent opticians or optometrists:** You may want to go this route if you have a strong or complicated prescription (if you wear progressive lenses, for instance). At retailers or independent opticians or optometrists, they can fit your frames and check to see exactly where you're looking through the lenses to find the PD, so they can be aligned precisely in the frames.

An optometrist (a doctor who performs routine eye exams and fits glasses) or optician (a technical specialist in fitting glasses) can help you select a pair that flatters your face shape and walk you through options for lenses.

Walmart Vision Center and Costco Optical both have licensed optometrists on-site and are likely to offer specs at much lower prices than you'll find at boutique opticians. The same goes for the big-chain vision centers, such as America's Best, LensCrafters, and Pearle Vision, which offer seasonal sales (savings of at least 20 percent on a pair of eyeglasses) and BOGO deals.

246. Keep your eyes peeled for price-match guarantees. Or try on glasses at a store, jot down the style number of the frames you fancy, and then search for a website that sells the same ones for less. You can also ask for a price break. It never hurts to ask for a discount or special deal on a second pair.

 247. Members and their families receive exclusive discounts at participating retailers and independent provider locations nationwide, as well as online, through AARP Vision Discounts provided by EyeMed. You save 50 percent on prescription lenses with the purchase of a frame at LensCrafters, 30 percent on a complete pair of glasses (frames and lenses) at Glasses.com, and $10 on a complete pair of glasses at Target Optical. Visit aarp.org/vision-discounts.

Hearing Better for Less

248. Hearing aids can sell at a retail markup of up to 117 percent. But those prices can be flexible. In one survey, about half of the 14 percent of people who haggled got a better deal. Or buy online: It can save you over $1,000 per pair.

249. If you have mild to moderate hearing loss, you may benefit from the new over-the-counter hearing aids, which are thousands of dollars cheaper than traditional prescription hearing aids. To find out more, see AARP's *Hearing Loss For Dummies* (published by Wiley).

250. Know what to look for when you buy hearing aids.

- **The words "over-the-counter (OTC) hearing aid" on the package:** This is the FDA-regulated designation that says you're purchasing actual hearing aids and not some type of amplification device. Several models may also carry the designation "Self-Fitting OTC Hearing Aid."

- **Requirements for smartphones:** Many, but not all, OTC hearing aids require users to download and use an app on their smartphone. For details about types compatible with your phone — some work only with iPhones, not Androids — you'll have to go to the maker's website or read the material inside the package.

- **A 30-day (or more) return policy:** The Hearing Loss Association of America recommends choosing devices with a generous return policy. It can take several weeks to know whether new hearing aids work for you, in part because your brain has to acclimate to all the new sounds you hear.

  You want to allow yourself time to get used to wearing a hearing aid and testing it out in different environments. Check out how different tips, domes, or petal sizes feel on models that have them, and which types feel more comfortable.

  Soundly founder Blake Cadwell, who wears hearing aids, says to make sure you have at least 45 days to check them out.

  You also want to ask about what kind of support is available once the trial expires, including the cost of replacing a damaged or lost hearing aid.

- **Added features:** More expensive OTCs work with telecoils, which pick up signals sent directly to your hearing aids in movie theaters and concert halls. Others may come with Bluetooth options that allow you to stream phone calls and other media wirelessly through your hearing aids.

Different hearing aid manufacturers market different features: models with more powerful speakers, processors, or directional microphones that can focus on the person you're talking with; features that can filter out background noise; and hearing aids that exploit the latest artificial intelligence technologies.

Some hearing aids can automatically adjust to different volumes at different frequencies. Premium models let you customize your hearing profile, typically via Bluetooth and a smartphone app.

- **Rechargeable versus battery-powered:** Choose a power option that allows you to wear hearing aids during all your waking hours. Your brain needs to receive input consistently to acclimate to the new device. More expensive models tend to include rechargeable batteries and sometimes wireless charging options. Generally, less expensive hearing aids require you to periodically replace the batteries.

- **A look that you like:** Hearing professionals say wearing your hearing aids regularly is crucial to making the most of them and may even protect hearing from further loss. So buying a look that you are comfortable with is important. Some hearing aids fit behind the ears or stick out some, while others sit inside your ears and have barely visible threads that help you remove the hearing aids.

 251. Save 20 percent on hearing aids and 15 percent on accessories with AARP Hearing Solutions provided by UnitedHealthcare Hearing. Members also get a hearing test at no cost and personalized support through a large nationwide network of hearing providers. Visit aarp.org/hearing-solutions.

 252. Take a confidential hearing test by phone once a year for free. The test is an independent and scientifically validated hearing screen test developed with funding from the National Institutes of Health. Visit aarp.org/hearing-test.

Tapping into Technology Bargains

You may be reading this on your phone, tablet, or computer. Or you may be reading this while checking your email or text or bingeing on your favorite show. Our gadgets have become a ubiquitous and indispensable part of life nearly every minute of every day. Here are ways to save on all the tech you and your family use.

Getting Deals on TVs, Laptops, Computers, and Other Gear

253. Know the best time to buy tech. TVs and cameras go on sale during the year-end holidays. Computer prices drop in late spring. Older devices often get discounted when new versions hit the store, usually in the fall.

254. Consider unfamiliar brands. *Consumer Reports*–recommended devices include lesser-known brands that can cost hundreds of dollars less than similar models from big names.

255. Know what to look for when buying a new computer. If you haven't bought one in three or more years, computers have changed quite a bit. Today's machines are generally faster, more power-efficient, thinner, and, in many cases, cheaper.

One thing that hasn't changed is the jargon that can still baffle buyers without advanced degrees or a passion for technology. Here's how to get the computer you need without paying for what you don't.

- **Processor speed:** This is the master chip that drives your computer. Current Windows-based computers typically run 10th- or 11th-generation Intel chips. Look for the model number (examples: i5 or i7), then find the two digits immediately after that, preferably 10 or 11.

- **Device types:** America has gone mobile, and so have computers. Laptops are the most popular type of computer today, followed by tablets. Together, portable devices account for about four-fifths of the worldwide market.

  Those big desktop boxes of old are still available but are usually built for high-end users who need ultra-high-speed capability. You can also hook up a laptop to a monitor on your desk when you need a larger display. They, too, have dropped substantially in cost; great monitors can be had for $150 or less.

- **RAM:** RAM is your computer's short-term memory — essentially, its operating workspace. The more RAM, the more programs or browser tabs you can have open and running smoothly at the same time and the fewer freeze-ups on your monitor. Experts recommend at least 8 gigabytes (GB) of RAM, though cloud-based Chromebooks can work well with just 4GB.

- **Cable connecters or wireless:** Those USB ports for power-cable and monitor connections are mostly gone. The new industry standard for connecting power-drawing accessories is the smaller USB-C. It can be used for anything.

  You may need an adapter to plug in older devices or accessories. You can get a hub that lets you plug several peripherals into one USB-C port starting at around $20. And many peripherals don't require plugging in at all. Since your last computer purchase, your keyboard, mouse, and printer have gone wireless, often via Bluetooth.

- **Cost:** You should be able to find a Windows laptop that costs less than $600 and should last up to five years. More expensive models should have more speed, memory, and storage. Macs start at about $900.

- **Screen size:** A larger screen makes reading and viewing easier. Whether you buy a monitor for a desktop computer or to hook up to a laptop, look for one that is 27 or 32 inches.

  The sweet spot for laptops is 14 or 15 inches, which balances readability, portability, space efficiency, and cost. Also, pay attention to screen resolution specifications. Choose a model with full HD (1080p) resolution; avoid 720p, below today's standards, or the new high-end 4K resolution displays, which curtail battery life.

- **Data storage:** A good starting point for internal storage is 256GB, but you can get by with less because of one big area of change in the past few years. Increasingly, computer users are storing documents, photos, and videos "in the cloud," which means on secure servers you subscribe to and access online.

  This reduces your need for a large hard drive inside your computer and lets you access your files from your mobile devices and other computers. Another benefit: When you buy a new computer, you won't need to transfer a mountain of data.

- **Audio and video:** Most computers sold today come with high-quality video and audio components — that is, built-in speakers, cameras, and microphones — and wireless Wi-Fi and Bluetooth capabilities. Salespeople may try to get you to invest in enhanced video cards, but they are primarily for hard-core gamers.

- **Disc drives:** Few laptops sold today have CD or DVD players because their uses have mostly gone away. Software is downloaded or even cloud-based, most music or videos today are streamed over the internet, and files are stored either on your hard drive or in the cloud. But if you require one, plug-in external CD-DVD players are available for less than $50.

- **Internet connection:** Video calls freezing up? The problem may be with your internet service or Wi-Fi connection. Investing in a better router, using a signal booster, or getting higher-speed internet service could enhance your computer's performance more than buying a higher-grade model.

256. Save up to 15 percent off remote and on-demand IT trouble-shooting for computers, laptops, mobile devices, and more from Norton Ultimate Help Desk. Visit aarp.org/norton-support.

257. Buy a refurbished computer. You probably won't find many of the latest models on the refurb market, but you'll save big bucks. Just be sure to check the warranty and return policy. Try sites like Amazon, Backmarket.com, Best Buy, DiscountComputerDepot.com, eBay, Gazelle.com, Refurb.me, Target, and Walmart.

258. Shop open-box items — display models or unused products returned to the retailer (but not returned to the factory like refurbished items). A MacBook Air, for example, was purchased in an open box for $230 less. You can find open-box tech at Amazon, Apple, Best Buy, eBay, Newegg, and Walmart. Check the warranty and return policy.

259. Look at a Chromebook. The rise of cloud-based computing has led to a new laptop subcategory: Chromebooks, made by various manufacturers. These units come with minimal internal storage and are typically less expensive and lighter than other laptops. The battery life also tends to be good. Chromebooks are best for uses involving an internet connection.

260. Consider downloading Apache OpenOffice, LibreOffice, or NeoOffice. Their free programs are usually able to open Excel, Microsoft Word, and PowerPoint files.

STUDENTS

261. Check electronics stores and manufacturers for back-to-school specials and discounts for students for hardware and software. Apple, Best Buy, Dell, Microsoft, and Samsung are just a few of the brands to look into.

262. Get cheap cables. Expensive electronics cables don't carry signals better than cheap ones, which hold up fine for home use. Shop at Best Buy, monoprice.com, or office supply stores to buy off-brand phone chargers or connector cables. They work as well as those from name brands.

Cutting Costs on Cellphones

263. Buy a smaller phone. If you're not watching many videos or using your phone for work, you may not need a 6-inch-plus screen. You'll save by going with a smaller device.

264. Switch to auto-pay. Some providers, including AT&T, T-Mobile, and Verizon, often offer discounts for setting up automatic payments. Bonus: You'll never get hit with a late fee again.

265. Join forces. They're called family plans, but you need not be family to share a nicely discounted multiuser plan. The issue: Only one person "owns" the account. So set up recurring payments to the person responsible for the bill to ensure all are paying their share.

266. Get a prepaid plan. These plans are cheaper than the standard "pay-after-the-month's-charges-get-tallied" plan, and they almost never require a contract. But they tend to have fewer perks (such as free subscriptions to a TV or music app). Also, some prepaid plans will slow data speed more often than postpaid ones.

267. Pass on phone insurance. Between the substantial monthly fees, often-large deductibles, and hidden clauses (for example, what type of phone they get to replace your device with), most experts say these are not a great value.

268. Members save $10 per line per month on the AT&T Unlimited Premium plan, plus up to $50 in waived activation and upgrade fees. Visit aarp.org/att.

269. Consumer Cellular provides 5 percent off monthly service and usage charges and 30 percent off select accessories for AARP members. Plans start at $20 per month and include free activation. No contract is required. Visit aarp.org/consumer-cellular or present your AARP membership card at Target stores, which sell Consumer Cellular.

270. Get cell service from a mobile online network operator such as Tello or Ting. You'll pay full price for your phone, but after that you can save about $30 per month over major carriers.

271. Reduce background data use. Some phone apps use data even when you are not using them. Go to Settings to turn off data to apps you rarely use. For iPhone, under Settings, go to Cellular. For Android, go to Network & Internet, select App Data Usage, tap an app, and toggle off Background Data.

272. Invest in a screen protector (often under $10) and a good case for your phone. According to one report, roughly 30 percent of U.S. smartphone owners have a cracked screen. That can mean needing a new phone much earlier than necessary or a $100-plus repair.

Saving on Streaming, Cable, and Internet Services

273. Rotate your premium subscriptions. Pick one streaming service, say Disney+, HBO Max, or Hulu, and subscribe only to that for a few months. Binge your favorite shows, then cancel the subscription and subscribe to another one for the next three months. The services will have new episodes by the time you return.

274. Share streaming services. Check your services' terms of use and ask your grown kids to do the same. Most allow sharing with a limited number of "household members" or "family members," but they usually don't define the terms. By coordinating with your family, you can slash what you are paying.

275. Get TV the old-fashioned way. You don't need an expensive cable or streaming package to get live television. Just install a $30 television antenna; it will get you access to television channels like ABC, NBC, CBS, and Fox.

276. Skip the router rental. Your internet provider may be charging you a monthly fee for your equipment — but you can buy your own modem and router and make up the cost in a year.

277. Cut the cord. According to a recent report, U.S. cord-cutters — those who have severed ties with traditional cable or satellite plans — now number over 50 million. But even if you haven't fully taken the plunge, you probably subscribe to at least one streaming platform, such as Amazon Prime Video, Hulu, or Netflix. The streaming revolution has led to an explosion of new content and saved many of us big bucks on cable bills, but let's face it: It can get complicated! These tips can help you make sense of the streamers, discover niche services to add to your bingeing repertoire, and hopefully save you some bucks.

- **Consider bundling.** Much like shopping at Costco or Sam's Club, there are deals to be had when you buy in bulk. Take, for instance, the Disney Bundle, which gets you access to Disney+, Hulu, and ESPN+ and can save you over a third of what you'd pay for three separate subscriptions. Similarly, you can bundle Paramount+ and Showtime, which also includes live access to your local CBS station and no ads on streaming content.

- **Check whether streaming is included with your cable subscription.** If you haven't officially cut the cord, there's a good chance that you may already have access to a few great streaming services. HBO, for one, offers HBO Max access to most of its existing customers. Showtime, similarly, provides most traditional subscribers access to its Showtime Anytime app.

- **Cut costs by sitting through a few commercials.** We're sure you've heard of the big three streamers (Amazon Prime Video, Hulu, and Netflix), but did you know there are a ton of free ad-supported options out there? So while you may have to watch a few commercials, you don't have to pay a dime. Think of the following sites as noncombatants in the streaming wars.

  The Roku Channel: You may be familiar with Roku as a streaming device, like an Amazon Fire TV Stick, but the brand also has a channel of free content, which includes original shows from the dearly departed Quibi app.

  Peacock: NBCUniversal's year-old streaming service includes a totally free tier, which offers access to movies, TV shows (including *Downton Abbey*), and Peacock originals, such as the *Punky Brewster* reboot. There's plenty to watch for free, but there's also a paid premium tier that allows you to unlock more content.

Pluto TV: While this free streaming service also includes a library of on-demand movies, such as the James Bond franchise, it's notable for its refreshingly old-school format. Meant to reduce decision fatigue, the service is set up like a traditional TV: You can flip through thematic channels (TV Land Sitcoms, Black Cinema) and drop in on whatever's playing. And because this is a digital library, if you like what you see, you can always restart from the beginning.

Sling Free: You'll find a robust collection of bingeable shows, such as *3rd Rock from the Sun, Grace Under Fire, 21 Jump Street,* and *The Commish,* plus movies and live news. The service also allows subscribers to add premium channels or rent first-run films.

Tubi: With more than 20,000 movies and TV series, Tubi calls itself the largest library of streaming content. It's recently started releasing original content, such as the adult animated series *The Freak Brothers,* which features the voices of Woody Harrelson, John Goodman, and Tiffany Haddish.

Amazon Freevee (previously IMDb TV): Launched in 2019, this ad-supported service is the streaming home of *Mad Men* and loads of TV classics, and it's branching out with new original shows, including the crime drama *Leverage: Redemption* and the *Judge Judy* follow-up, *Judy Justice.*

Vudu: You can buy or rent films from this Fandango-owned streaming service, but the site also offers a selection of free options; the choices may not be as A-list as those found on some other streamers, but you can still find hidden gems such as *Carol, Pumping Iron,* and *Melancholia.*

- **See whether your mobile provider has any partnership deals.** Your cellphone plan may include complimentary subscriptions to streaming services. A number of the country's top providers have exclusive partnerships that could end up saving you quite a bit of money. Depending on their plan, some T-Mobile customers get access to Netflix, Paramount+, and Apple TV+. Sprint Unlimited includes a Hulu subscription, and eligible AT&T Unlimited plans come with HBO Max. Finally, many Verizon Wireless customers can get the entire Disney Bundle, a year of Discovery+, and 6 to 12 months of AMC+.

- **Focus on the entertainment you love.** Services such as Netflix and Amazon Prime Video boast expansive content libraries that can often feel overwhelming when you're trying to pick something to watch. If you find yourself gravitating toward the same types of content every night (say, documentaries or arthouse films), you may want to consider switching to a more niche streaming service dedicated to a specific genre. Options include the Criterion Channel ($10.99 a month), featuring more than 1,000 classic and contemporary films; Shudder ($5.99 a month), focused on horror and the supernatural; Dekkoo ($9.99 a month), for LGBTQ-themed movies, shorts, and TV shows; and ALLBLK ($5.99 a month), offering "entertainment that's inclusively, but unapologetically, Black."

- **Take advantage of the public library.** If you're a member of your local library, you may already have access to a free streaming service called Kanopy, which offers thousands of movies, including *Moonlight, Chinatown, Breathless,* and *Parasite*. You can also search a catalog of early films, including Fritz Lang's *Metropolis,* Charlie Chaplin's *Modern Times,* and Buster Keaton's *The General.* Not every public library system in the United States subscribes to the service, so be sure to chat with your librarian or check whether you have access on the website.

Tech to Save You Money

278. Stop paying for subscriptions you forgot you had. Apps such as Mint, Rocket Money, and Trim gather information on all of your subscriptions (including anything tech-related) and present them to you. That makes it easy to see what you're already paying for. Decide you are done with a subscription? Some apps will cancel it on your behalf.

279. Instead of using up your data, tap into the nearest Wi-Fi when you can. But be safe: Don't shop or bank over Wi-Fi; fraud criminals can intercept passwords and other sensitive data.

280. Avoid using your Wi-Fi to play games or stream music and movies if you're on a limited data plan. Those activities are data hogs that can quickly trigger charges.

281. Apps such as Data Usage, My Data Manager, and your wireless phone app can identify which of your actions eat up most data and alert you when you're near the limit.

282. Bundle. Take the free quiz at MyBundle.TV to discover the best options for television platforms that include the channels and features you want, as well as options to get the best value with most of those channels. In addition to those platforms, the site analyzes eight or more live, ad-supported TV services that range in price from $5 to $105 per month.

283. Get expert budget picks. *Consumer Reports* as well as websites like Reviewed.com and TheWirecutter.com review home tech gear. Along with their top-rated items, they usually include a budget pick.

Going Out without Breaking the Bank

D on't scrimp on fun! If you love sporting events, movies, plays, dance performances, or concerts, read on. Our experts offer tips for having fun for less.

Pinching Pennies at the Movies

284. Buy movie tickets in multiples. It's a great way to save if you live in a city known for inflated ticket prices. Look for them at wholesale retailers like Costco or buy straight from the movie theater's corporate website. Some corporations even offer discounted bulk ticket sales to their employees, so check your benefits package.

285. Don't pay fees for movie tickets. Some online sellers charge "convenience" fees of $1.50 to $2 or more per ticket. Bypass them by buying at the box office or from a no-fee online vendor.

MILITARY & VETERANS

286. Active-duty and retired military and their dependents may be eligible for a discount at Cinemark Theatres box offices at certain times or on certain days. Call your theater for details. Active and retired military members also qualify for a discount at some Regal Cinemas locations. Call your local theater for details and availability.

287. Enjoy at-home movie night. AARP Movies for Grownups regularly offers virtual screenings, from documentaries to classic films and recently released titles. Screenings are free for members and nonmembers, but advanced registration is required. To see what's coming up, visit https://watch.aarp.org/aarpmfg. For more movies, AARP Members Only Access features a rotating roster of full-length films and documentaries on-demand. Visit www.aarp.org/moa.

Saving on Sporting Events

288. Take in a minor league baseball game. Minor league games offer plenty of thrills, plus perks like activities and giveaways for kids. The cost to attend a game with the family is less than half of what it costs at a major league park. Go to milb.com to find a nearby minor league stadium. Or attend the big football championship or other sporting event at the local high school and cheer for the home team.

289. Attend spring training. See how your favorite baseball players work with their coaches — for free! Check out spring trainingconnection.com or mlb.com/spring-training/ballparks for locations and schedules.

290. Share season tickets. Arrange with your seat neighbors to trade tickets you can't use. You could save hundreds of dollars on a pair of NFL tickets.

291. See big games and big names for less. The average price of an NFL ticket was $108 in 2021, according to Statista. NBA tickets cost $85 to $95. Concerts cost an average of $96 in 2019, according to the latest data available from Statista, and big names can run way higher.

But you don't always have to pay that much to see your favorite team or artist. Here are five tips for saving money when you're trying to get a glimpse of the sports and music stars live and up close.

- **Wait.** Normally, you can get the best prices when they first go on sale at the box office. Many times, however, tickets sell out within a few minutes, and that's often because ticket resellers snatch them up for resale. If you can't get tickets from the primary source — the box office — then you have to buy them on the secondary market, via resellers such as Gametime, SeatGeek, or StubHub.

  The longer you wait, the cheaper the ticket gets, as sellers become nervous that they will get stuck with worthless inventory. If you buy NFL tickets 30 days before the game, you can expect to pay 10 percent more than average, but the prices will be 40 percent less than average the day before kickoff, according to Gametime.

- **Wait until the last minute.** Because you can often download tickets onto your smartphone, you can sometimes get great deals by waiting until just an hour before the event starts, when the brokers and suppliers unload inventory that will soon be worthless.

  Buy from a reputable ticket reseller rather than some guy in front of the concert hall or stadium, who may be selling fakes. Many resellers offer money-back guarantees that your seat is genuine. The risk is that you won't get the seat you wanted. If you just *have* to be in the front row, be prepared to pay for it. On the other hand, you can often have as much fun in the upper deck as you can up close and personal.

- **Swing by the actual box office.** Venues often hold back tickets for promoters as well as the artists and their guests, according to Stadium Help, a website for helping ticket buyers. If the box office has unused promotional tickets, they will sell them close to the time of the event. You never know, and it doesn't hurt to ask.

- **Use credit card points.** Some major credit-card companies, such as American Express and Citi, sometimes offer tickets at box-office prices before they are on sale to the general public — and you can use points to buy them, according to Stadium Help. Sometimes you need a presale code to take advantage of credit-card deals. This often is the support phone number on the back of the card or the first six digits of your card.

- **Be a fan.** Many artists have fan clubs, and they sometimes offer presale codes that let you buy tickets before they're for sale to the general public. Some artists charge to join their fan club: Eric Clapton, for example, charges up to $75 annually. You'll have to decide whether the fan-club cost is worth getting the presale tickets and other benefits, such as newsletters. Other fan sites, such as the one for country star Darius Rucker, are free.

  Sports teams have fan clubs, too. The San Francisco Giants, for example, offer membership to The 415, which includes access to a special section 415 feet from home plate — as well as discounted ticket offers. Again, you have to weigh the cost of the club against the benefits of discounted tickets.

Enjoying Concerts, Theater, and Dance Performances on the Cheap

292. AARP members save on tickets to select shows and events from Ticketmaster. Offers include 2-for-1 tickets and events with select tickets under $40. Subject to availability, venue, and artist restrictions. Conditions apply. For details, visit aarp.org/ticketmaster.

293. Look out for summer concerts or music festivals at county and state fairs around your region every summer. Sometimes you can get free lawn seats or save with early bird discounts.

294. Check out your local open mic. Enjoy great music without forking over $50 (or more!) for a concert ticket. Open mics are free or cheap. Some performers are diamonds in the rough, but that's part of the fun.

295. Check on campus for concerts. If you live near a college town, you can catch big-name acts cheap. Artists and performers often include campus theaters as part of their concert tours, and tickets may go for less than they would in a stadium or theater in a major city.

296. Skip the cover charge. Big-city dwellers can often find live music at restaurants in nearby small towns without paying at the door. For the price of dinner, you get an evening of music.

297. Attend open rehearsals for the ballet, opera, plays, or the symphony. Depending on the venue, rehearsals may be free or at substantially reduced ticket prices.

298. Volunteer to usher at local theaters. You'll get the satisfaction of helping out while also getting to see performances for free. What's more, think of the bragging rights that come from supporting your local arts.

299. Catch a pre-Broadway show. Check industry sites like broadway.com and broadwayworld.com to know when a Broadway show may be headed your way for a tour or out-of-town tryout. And when in New York, check broadwayforbrokepeople.com, a guide to getting great tickets for less than the usual prices.

MILITARY & VETERANS

300. Veterans, service members, and Gold Star families can find free and discounted tickets to a variety of events. Visit www.vettix.org/partner/veteransaffairs.

Tech to Save You Money

301. Monitor discount ticket apps and websites. Several digital businesses offer theater, concert, comedy club, and other cultural event tickets at big discounts and are worth monitoring. They include Goldstar, Groupon, and TodayTix. Sites may also offer discounts for activities like bowling and escape rooms.

302. Whatever entertainment you choose, save on your evening expenses by dining during happy hour rather than peak dinner hours or later, and you'll save around 35 percent on food and 20 percent on drinks. Check your neighborhood establishments to find out when they host happy hour, or use a site like happable.com or https://happyhournearme.com to get details on happy hour deals at local restaurants.

303. Find AARP member discounts for local entertainment at memberoffers.aarp.org/entertainment or on the AARP Now app.

Studying Education Costs

The cost of education is rising, but don't let that temper your zeal for learning. Whether you're fresh out of school or looking to switch careers later in life, our experts offer tips for saving thousands of dollars.

Keeping Tuition Low

304. Let your job send you to school. Around half of employers offer college education assistance, and you may not even need to be studying something directly linked to your work. Generally, you don't have to pay federal income tax on the first $5,250 of assistance.

305. Sign up for free or mostly free massive open online courses (MOOCs) through portals such as Coursera (www.coursera.org/), eX (www.edx.org), and LinkedIn Learning (www.linkedin.com/learning).

These classes cover an expansive array of subjects from animation to IT to zoology. You can find thousands of classes and degree and certificate programs, according to Class Central (classcentral.com), which has a searchable database.

MOOCs were initially offered by universities that wanted to openly share their courses with a mass audience. Now, universities such as Duke, Harvard, MIT, Stanford, and Yale produce these courses, along with nonprofits, trade groups, and companies such as Google and Microsoft.

306. Join an interactive class or lecture on AARP's Virtual Community Center, free for members and nonmembers alike. Browse the calendar by date or explore categories to find the experience right for you. Visit local.aarp.org/ virtual-community-center/.

307. Take advantage of tax credits for school. The American Opportunity Tax Credit is good for four years of higher education, with a maximum annual credit of $2,500. There's also the Lifetime Learning Tax Credit, which is worth up to $2,000 per tax return, with an unlimited number of years. Unlike deductions, which reduce your taxable income (and therefore your taxes), tax credits reduce your tax bill dollar for dollar.

308. Look at community colleges, where tuition is thousands of dollars per year lower than four-year schools. Some students start with two years of community college and then transfer to a four-year school.

OLDER ADULTS

309. If you're an older student, ask at community and four-year colleges whether they offer special programs or free or reduced tuition fees. In fact, some institutions even translate life experience into academic credits, which can shorten your academic timeline — and lessen your financial investment.

310. Interested in learning but don't need a full-fledged degree? Many institutions allow students and even community members to audit classes for free on a space-available basis. Ask about specific residency, age, and other requirements at schools in your area.

Seeking Financial Assistance

311. Use the Savi Student Loan Repayment Tool to see whether you qualify for student loan forgiveness or lower monthly payments. Get a free repayment and forgiveness eligibility review, plus, if you need more help, AARP members and their families can save up to $50 off of Savi Essential or Savi Pro services, which include customized support. Visit aarp.org/savi-tool.

**MILITARY &
VETERANS**

312. Substantial financial help is available for survivors of service members interested in pursuing education or vocational training. In some cases, the government will pay all or a large part of tuition costs for college and other educational programs.

Two key programs that eligible surviving spouses and children should explore are the Fry Scholarship (www. va.gov/education/survivor-dependent-benefits/ fry-scholarship/) and Survivors' and Dependents' Educational Assistance (DEA) (www.va.gov/education/ survivor-dependent-benefits/dependents-education-assistance/).

Under the Fry program, the government pays the full cost of in-state tuition at public institutions, or up to about $26,000 a year for a private school, plus a monthly housing allowance and a stipend for books and supplies. This scholarship, paid directly to the school, was expanded to include surviving spouses in 2014.

Eligible survivors who choose the DEA program instead of the Fry scholarship can get a monthly check sent directly to them to pay educational costs. The maximum amount for full-time students currently is about $1,400 per month.

The DEA and Fry programs can be used for college, vocational and business technical programs, apprenticeship programs, certification tests, and tutoring.

The federal Forever GI Bill, enacted in 2017, has made it easier for survivors to transfer benefits under the GI Bill after the death of service members.

Eligibility for educational benefits can depend on a number of factors, including the date and circumstances of a veteran's death, the ages of dependent children, and the widow or widower's marital status.

313. Refinance student loans. Cutting a few percentage points off a large loan can save you thousands over time. Many banks now offer refinancing options. Note that you may sacrifice eligibility for any government loan forgiveness programs if you do this.

314. Apply for student aid, no matter your age. You can seek loans, grants, and scholarships whether you are starting out in college or want to burnish your credentials or pivot careers and pursue a second act.

Student aid is so associated with young kids coming straight out of high school that you may write it off as a possibility. But that's a mistake — you are absolutely eligible, no matter your age or stage of life.

Start where every other college student does: Fill out the FAFSA. The Free Application for Federal Student Aid (fafsa. gov) is the master key that helps unlock loans and grants at the federal, state, and institutional levels. Anyone over the age of 24 is considered "independent," which means no parental informational is required.

Once you fill out and submit the FAFSA, you will receive a package of loans and grants.

You can fill out the FAFSA even in your current school year. So if you are already enrolled and taking courses, you can still file all the way through June 30 of your current school year. Similarly, if you are looking to start school the following fall, your deadline is June 30 of that school year. The form then has to be filled out every year.

That being said, early application is always the better strategy, because some pots of student money will run out. For example, Alaska, Illinois, Kentucky, Missouri, Nevada, North Carolina, North Dakota, Oklahoma, Oregon, South Carolina, Texas, Vermont, and Washington all award state aid on a first-come, first-served basis until the money is depleted.

If you're unhappy with the aid assistance you receive, you can always appeal. Because income information is based on prior years, an appeal may succeed if there have been recent changes to your financial status — a layoff, for instance.

Keep in mind that federal Pell Grants are only for the first bachelor's degree — so if you're pursuing a second bachelor's, you're not eligible for Pell Grants. For that reason, you may want to consider going to graduate school instead of getting a second undergraduate degree.

In addition to federal, state, and institutional aid, you can also search for scholarships at fastweb.com, finaid.org, and other sites, some of which are specifically designed for mature students. Enter your information and be matched with opportunities among databases of more than 1.5 million scholarships and billions of dollars in funding.

Finally, check to see whether your state offers financial aid — almost every state does. You can find information on your state programs through the National Association of Student Financial Aid Administrators (www.nasfaa.org).

Cutting Travel Expenses

Travel costs can add up, whether you're going near or far, for a vacation, a family visit, or work. But for each step of the way, we offer money-saving tips, from packing and planning to flying, lodging, and fun.

Getting Ready for Your Trip

315. For less than $30, you can buy a set of zip-up compression bags that allow you to squeeze more clothes into your carry-on and bypass costly checked luggage. These airtight bags also keep you wrinkle-free and organized. Just stack like items, roll or fold them, and slide them into a bag. Even cheaper: Substitute fancy compression bags for the gallon-size, see-through, resealable zippered plastic storage bags.

316. Pack pieces of clothing that mix and match and multitask. Think neutral — black, navy, khaki, tan — and add a pop of bright color. Take underwear for each day, but limit shoes to a pair of walkable everyday shoes, a pair of dressier shoes, and if it's summer, sandals.

317. Buy luggage in March. Travel retailers know we gear up for spring and summer vacations in March, so they often discount prices.

318. Purchase an international phone/data package before you leave to prevent costly roaming charges. Every phone carrier offers its customers international plans, which vary. For Verizon and AT&T customers, for instance, overseas options include a $10 per day plan for unlimited calls, text, and data. Check to make sure the plan covers your destinations.

You can also buy a prepaid SIM card. A SIM card stores your subscriber data in your phone. When you're traveling internationally, you can replace it with a card that gives you a local phone number. The first necessary step: Ask your carrier to "unlock" your phone. The unlocking process varies depending on the phone and the carrier; some new phones are unlocked by default.

You can buy a SIM card for your destination before you leave. (Before you buy, research the most used networks in the country you're visiting and buy that brand of SIM card. In France, for example, the largest mobile company is Orange, followed by SFR and Bouygues Télécom.) The cards vary based on the amount of data, minutes, texts, and the number of countries where you can use them. You can install the card after you land by following instructions that are included with it.

Another option is to buy a SIM card at your destination — such as from a mobile provider at the airport or a local department store. The upside of buying it when you arrive is that a store employee can help you choose the right data plan, install the card, and make sure it's the right one for your phone.

319. Plan ahead for how you'll pay when you're away. Contact your credit- and debit-card companies in advance to tell them when and where you'll be traveling — so they don't stop payment on your purchases — and find out whether they charge a foreign transaction fee. Try to use cards that don't assess the fee, which can be as high as 3 percent. When you purchase items while away, put the transaction through in local currency, not U.S. dollars, to save up to 20 percent.

You probably don't need to bring local currency with you. It's often cheaper to withdraw cash from a local ATM. You'll usually best to avoid those currency exchange booths in foreign countries, which tend to charge much higher fees.

320. Drive, don't fly, if your trip is less than 500 miles away. You can potentially save thousands of dollars by not buying plane tickets — and you'll have your car and gear with you. And a road trip won't add much time by the time you factor in driving to and from the airport and waiting for your flight (not to mention flight delays!).

321. Organize your vacation. With TripIt, forward all your confirmation emails — for flights, hotels, rental cars, and tickets — to plans@tripit.com, and the service will organize everything into a detailed summary, complete with confirmation codes, maps, and other info. The convenient one-stop app holds important details of your trip. The optional TripIt Pro, a premium $49-a-year service, has extras including real-time flight alerts and info on alternate flights if yours is delayed or canceled. Expedia Trip Planner and TripAdvisor offer similar services.

Taking Flights

322. Search for flights using flexible dates and airports. Shifting an arrival or departure date by a single day may save you a surprisingly large amount of cash. Many flight search engines show lower-priced options. You'll also find that some new, small, and low-cost carriers often use secondary nearby airports instead of the city's main airport.

323. Fly from hubs. Airlines use hub airports to consolidate planes and save costs. Fares are cheaper and stopovers are rare when you fly between hubs. It may make sense to drive to a hub.

MILITARY & VETERANS

324. Many U.S. airlines offer a military discount or incentive, such as checked bag fee waivers or seat upgrades. Visit the airline's website or call its customer service department to find out more. Airline discounts may only apply to active-duty, National Guard, or reserve service members — and they may only apply when traveling on orders.

325. Fly when everyone else isn't. In a typical week, this would be a Tuesday or Wednesday, when, according to one airfare prediction app, travelers save an average of 10 percent on domestic tickets compared with weekend dates. During the holiday period, avoid the few days before and after major holidays.

326. Don't procrastinate purchasing your ticket. In general, travelers who began searching for flights on Hopper 90 days in advance of their trips saved 31 percent more on domestic trips than those who waited until three weeks before departure.

327. British Airways offers $65 to $200 off roundtrip tickets purchased online for AARP members. Visit aarp.org/british-airways for details.

328. Parking at the airport? AARP members can save on reservations made at any of Park Ride Fly USA's off-airport parking locations nationwide. Visit aarp.org/park-ride-fly.

329. Consider new airlines. Two airlines — Avelo and Breeze — launched during the pandemic and another, Northern Pacific Airways, is slated to start flying at press time. New airlines like these often have a strategy of winning market share by offering ultra-low fares. One caution: These airlines tend to highlight base fares for tickets, so make sure you understand the total cost before making the purchase.

330. Watch existing airlines on the same routes. As start-up airlines add new routes, established airlines flying those routes often lower their prices amid the increased competition.

331. Book your group members separately. Airlines often have a certain number of seats available at each pricing level. If they only have three tickets available at $200, and you're trying to buy four seats at once, they won't turn up in your search. Book individually or in groups of two. You could nab the low-price seats.

332. Use your airline card to save on other expenses. In addition to racking up miles, paying for a flight with an airline credit card may offer unexpected savings on travel like a free checked bag or discounts on in-flight food and drink.

333. Make a stop. Direct flights cost, on average, 20 percent more than those with a layover, according to Google Flights. If you aren't pressed for time, you can make a layover more palatable by downloading apps where you can find things to do at the airport, like shopping tips or restaurant recommendations.

Using Rental Cars and Trains

334. Choose a car rental location near, not at, the airport, for a lower rental rate.

335. AARP members save up to 30 percent off base rates and receive a 3 percent credit to apply to rentals within 12 months, plus a free upgrade on compact through full-size car class bookings when available, and an additional driver at no cost at Avis and Budget. Visit aarp.org/car-rentals.

336. Skip rental car insurance. Most of the time you already have adequate coverage through your personal insurance.

337. Plan to rent a car on vacation? Pack your toll pass transponder device; many can be used at toll plazas in other states. In Illinois, for example, vehicles with an I-PASS device pay half of what the cash lane charges.

OLDER ADULTS

338. Amtrak cuts 10 percent off most fares for riders 62-plus. Visit www.amtrak.com/deals-discounts/everyday-discounts/seniors-discount.html.

Via Rail Canada offers 10 percent off adult fares for travelers over 60. Visit www.viarail.ca/en/offers/senior.

339. First-class train tickets in Europe cost up to twice as much as those in second class, with a minimal difference in comfort.

OLDER ADULTS

340. Use your age. Seniors traveling by train can find ticket deals, most of which require a discount card purchased at train stations in Europe (discounts start between ages 60 and 67).

Looking for Less Expensive Lodging

341. Book hotels last minute, if you can. For example, if you're planning a road trip and you're flexible about where to stay, you'll save an average of 13 percent by booking two weeks in advance rather than four months out, a NerdWallet study reveals.

342. AARP members save up to 20 percent off stays at major hotels such as Best Western, Choice Hotels, Hilton, IHG Hotels & Resorts, and Wyndham. Visit aarp.org/hotel-discounts.

343. Blind-book a hotel. Tell Hotwire.com or Priceline.com the neighborhood, star rating, and amenities you want, and you'll save up to 60 percent if you book before knowing the name of the hotel.

344. For weekend travel, stay in a business hotel. The road warriors are gone and so are the high prices. These hotels will be in the business district — which isn't always the most vibrant part of town — but that's a small trade-off if you're getting a good deal.

345. Avoid conventions. Cities like Washington, D.C., Las Vegas, and Orlando have the best hotel rates when no conventions are in town. Check out a city's official tourism website under Convention Calendar to spot the best times for a visit.

346. Get hotel deals at Hotels.com, the oldest hotel-booking service and website. Its popular app benefits from an intuitive interface, maps and rideshare integration, support for smartwatches, a "secret price" feature, and one of the best loyalty and rewards programs, including a "stay 10 nights and get the next one free" feature.

To reduce the likelihood of fake reviews, all customers who rate or review a hotel must have stayed there.

And then Pruvo helps you get a better price on your hotel after you've booked it. You read that correctly.

Book your hotel room however you like, and forward the confirmation email to save@pruvo.com. If the hotel drops the rate on the room — a very common occurrence — you'll be notified about how much you'll save and instructed on how to cancel the original reservation and rebook at the lower rate. Rebooking is optional.

Also consider EVHotels (www.evhotels.org) to find hotels with electric vehicle chargers, and HotelTonight (hoteltonight.com), which, contrary to its name, allows bookings 100 days in advance of your check-in date.

347. Don't pay resort fees. About 40 percent of luxury hotels now charge these fees for facilities like pools or concierge services, which average about $25 per night. Look for lodging without the extra charge at ResortFeeChecker.com. Another tactic to avoid these fees: Book with hotel loyalty points. Hilton Honors and World of Hyatt are among the loyalty programs that often waive resort fees.

348. Hostels — for people of all ages — offer private rooms and baths at a fraction of the cost of what you'd pay at a chain hotel, and many offer amenities like gyms and saunas. Check Booking.com/hostels, Hostelworld.com, or Hostelz.com to see what's available.

349. Consider looking into HouseCarers.com ($50 annual fee) or MindMyHouse.com ($20 annual fee) to stay rent free in homes all over the globe. The arrangement may also include pet care or light housework. The site TrustedHouseSitters.com matches travelers with people who need their pets and homes watched. Save on a hotel room and make a furry friend.

350. Some foreign universities rent rooms to summer travelers while their students are away on break. Go to UniversityRooms.com.

351. If hotel rates seem sky-high, consider finding lodging on sites like airbnb.com, homestay.com, and vrbo.com; you'll often pay less and feel like a local.

352. When you're booking a room at a hotel, ask whether it offers military discounts. Most hotel chains offer reduced rates.

MILITARY & VETERANS

Eating Good Food for Less

353. Skip the hotel concierge when in search of good, inexpensive restaurant meals. Ask locals where to eat. Just pop into a shop and ask a clerk. You'll get a more authentic experience while saving money.

354. "Restaurant Weeks" are held during a city's slack season for tourism. You can eat at top restaurants for a fraction of the regular cost. Be sure to reserve early.

355. If you want to try an expensive restaurant on vacation, do so for lunch. Often the menu is the same as the dinner menu, but prices may be 25 percent less.

356. Every country has its equivalent of the hot dog stand, where you can grab a filling and inexpensive bite — French crêperies, Greek souvlaki stands, Danish pølse (sausage) vendors, Italian pizza rustica takeout shops, and Dutch herring carts.

Sightseeing at Your Destination

357. Many museums have designated days when they offer free admission. Call them or check their websites to find out your options.

358. Check out Freetour.com, Free Tours by Foot (freetours byfoot.com), and GuruWalk (www.guruwalk.com) to find tours you can take in cities across the globe. The sites offer pay-what-you-like guided tours, and some provide links to self-guided tours as well.

359. Visit internationalgreeter.org/ to find out about taking tours with local guides. There's also NewEuropeTours.eu, which offers no-cost city walking tours with locals in Europe and Israel. In the United States, call the chamber of commerce in your destination.

360. Sightseeing passes can steer travelers to attractions they don't care to see. Save money by avoiding packages with costly sightseeing passes — unless you love to visit three museums in one day!

 361. Grand European Travel offers AARP members $100 off per person on more than 300 guided vacations and river cruises throughout Europe and destinations around the world, even U.S. national parks. Visit aarp.org/grand-european.

362. On a handful of days each year, national parks that typically charge an entrance fee allow free admission to all visitors. Days include the anniversary of the Great American Outdoors Act (August 4), National Public Lands Day (September 24), and Veterans Day (November 11).

OLDER ADULTS

363. Buy a lifetime park pass. There are 63 official national parks in the United States, but the National Park Service oversees 423 sites, including many that are far less visited than big-name parks. A lifetime park pass ($80 for those over 62) gets you into all of them.

364. Find no-cost attractions. Why pay admission to see a cave, waterfall, or pretty vista if there are similar ones nearby that are free? Before you get in line, check online maps or chat with a local to find a similar activity that's off the beaten path.

365. For road travelers in the United States and Canada, Roadtrippers.com lets you discover millions of places along your route, whether you need a great restaurant, a recommended motel or hotel, a national park, quirky roadside attractions, or other points of interest. Plan, save, and share your trip itinerary with family and friends. Roadside America and Wanderlog offer similar services.

Timing Your Trip to Save Big Bucks

366. Go off-season and reap rewards like long walks on a deserted beach, great restaurants without a reservation, and no traffic jams, not to mention cost savings. Off-season travel is not only cheaper, but it can also be more relaxing than fighting in-season crowds. For example, a two-bedroom oceanfront condo on the Outer Banks of North Carolina is $200 per night in April, but the cost shoots up in June.

367. Head to ski resorts in the summer and beach locations in late August or early September.

368. Have your weekends on Wednesdays and Thursdays. Most resorts and inns offer lower rates on weekdays than on weekends, so you can save more by going midweek. Some resorts offer better prices on Sunday-through-Thursday packages.

Tech to Save You Money

369. Visit the AARP Travel site (aarp.org/travel) for ideas on your next trip, whether or not you're an AARP member. Find out where to stay and eat, book your hotel and travel, and discover the latest deals.

370. Use your smartphone to communicate in a language you don't know. Apple Translate, available only on iOS devices, currently can translate 18 languages; Google Translate, 133 languages; and iTranslate Translator, more than 100 languages.

You can use your smartphone's microphone for speech translation. Some apps allow bilingual conversations, have handwriting support, contain quick-access phrasebooks, and even boast an augmented reality feature that will instantly translate text in images — just point your phone's camera at a sign, menu, or photo.

371. When booking through the AARP Travel Center Powered by Expedia, AARP members get exclusive savings on hotels, car rentals, cruises, and vacation packages. Visit aarp.org/expedia-discounts.

Enjoying Hobbies for Less

P ursuing hobbies doesn't have to cost a lot. Our experts offer many ways to have fun indoors and out — often for free!

Reading for Less

372. Get free e-books at the library! Download the Libby app to get thousands of e-books, audiobooks, and magazines from your public library. More than 90 percent of libraries work with the app. You can read works within the app or send them to your Kindle. All you need to do is download the Libby app from your app store and then log in with your library credentials. For assistance, just take your device into the library and ask a librarian for help.

You can also download nearly 60,000 public domain e-books, including many classics and favorites, at Project Gutenberg, a free library, at gutenberg.org. You can search by title or author. For suggestions, click Frequently Downloaded. To read on a computer, tablet, or phone, click Read This Book Online: HTML, and the pages will pop up on your screen. No special software or apps are needed.

Or check out the World Digital Library at www.loc.gov/collections/world-digital-library, a project of the Library of Congress to preserve and share significant historical and cultural documents. The collection includes more than 12,000 publications dating as far back as 8000 BCE.

373. You can join AARP's Book of the Month, which curates new books every month and lets you pick one to have delivered straight to your door. After signing up, AARP members get one book for $5, a free gift, and a free book annually. Visit aarp.org/botm.

374. To find free samples on Goodreads, where bookworms rate and review books, click on the title of a book and then click Preview. To search for free e-books and more excerpts, go to www.goodreads.com/ebooks?sort=readable. One wrinkle: Some titles may have been free when a fan listed them but are no longer available. Or on Amazon, click on "Look inside" on select books to get a preview.

375. If you're an Amazon Prime member who loves trying new authors but doesn't have the patience to browse, sign up for Amazon Prime Reads and you'll get a steady supply of books. Each month, you'll receive an email with a selection of free options. You can download one or two of them straight to your Kindle or Kindle app. It's a nice perk of your Prime membership.

376. Swap books with friends, neighbors — or strangers! At BookMooch.com, you can list books you want to get rid of and get points when you send them to people who request them. Use the points to order used books.

You can join an online book-swapping club like PaperBackSwap (www.paperbackswap.com/index.php), which lets you exchange books with other readers for the cost of postage.

377. Many libraries sell donated books to raise funds. You can often find like-new recent titles at a low cost — and support your library at the same time.

378. AARP Members Only Access features full book serials and interviews with authors. Visit www.aarp.org/moa.

Gardening While Growing Your Savings

379. Regrow veggies. Cut green onions an inch from their roots and submerge in water, and they'll regrow. Do the same with romaine lettuce, cabbage, basil, celery, onions, and even pineapples; then transfer the plants to a pot of soil once the leaves start to appear.

380. Plant edible perennials. Many herbs and spices — among them garlic, rosemary, thyme, and oregano — will grow back year after year, making them a great value. Plus, they are often easy to grow because deer and other critters won't eat them. Several of these do great in pots outside the kitchen door, so you don't even need a garden.

381. Order bare-root plants. These are trees, shrubs, berries, and perennials that are sold in a dormant state with no soil on the roots. They are a lot lighter to ship than plants growing in soil and therefore less expensive to purchase online. Their light weight makes planting much easier on your back, and the hole you have to dig can be smaller.

382. Look for disease resistance. Planting varieties that are genetically resistant to disease can save you a bundle that you'd otherwise spend on pesticides and replacing dead plants. Some online catalogs will let you sort by "disease resistance."

383. Plant strategically. Grow the more expensive fruits and vegetables your family likes. Plant more high-value crops like garlic, arugula, and strawberries.

384. Hold a seed swap. Unless you have a truly large garden, you'll rarely use up a full packet of seeds. And it's always best to plant seeds the same year you purchase them, rather than store them for future seasons. The solution: Connect with neighbors or friends who garden, and coordinate your seed-buying — with the goal of sharing packets and cutting costs.

385. Join a community garden, or if there are none nearby, collaborate with neighbors to start one. You can have fun and save money on store-bought produce. Find tips on the American Community Gardening Association website (www. communitygarden.org).

386. An unsung hero in the gardener's arsenal is the local extension service. Each of the 50 states has a cooperative extension system, and most answer questions via a hotline and offer soil testing and pest identification for free or at a nominal cost. You can find your nearest extension service on the U.S. Department of Agriculture's Land Grant Directory (www.nifa.usda.gov/land-grant-colleges-and-universities-partner-website-directory); click on your state and then choose "extension" in the drop-down menu.

Garden-focused podcasts also offer a wealth of expertise and advice on the topic. (Side benefit: They can be listened to while pulling weeds!)

Garden shops are also helpful. And big-box garden stores often have great deals because they buy in bulk.

Trying Other Fun Pastimes

387. Join AARP's community of 50,000-plus volunteers and donate your time and talent — in person or from home — to improve the lives of others. Visit www.aarp.org/volunteer.

388. Love yoga? Try classes online, or on June 20, the International Day of Yoga, check local studios for free classes.

389. Find free 5-minute yoga routines from Larry Payne, founding president of the International Association of Yoga Therapists. Visit www.aarp.org/moa and search for "yoga."

390. At ancestry.com, AARP members save 30 percent on the first year of an All Access or a World Explorer subscription and get access to records and online tools to search, save, and share their family history. If you're new to Ancestry, you'll receive the discount on the first year of your subscription only. If you already have an Ancestry account, you'll receive the discount when you renew your subscription for a year.

391. Throw an artist party. Buy inexpensive watercolors, paper, and brushes and have your guests paint a still life. Compare results, laugh, and enjoy!

392. Many golf courses have military discounts. Ask your favorite courses to see what they offer.

393. Take a brewery tour. With the growth of craft beers, many cities now have breweries that offer free or low-cost tours. Similar tours may be offered by other manufacturers, such as a whiskey distillery, a chocolate maker, or a potato chip manufacturer. Frequently, free samples are given out at the tour's end.

394. Cooking schools run restaurants where students get hands-on training, and the public gets to eat without paying top-chef prices.

395. Find free online games to play at games.aarp.org/. Have fun and challenge your brain!

396. Go back to the future. Board games were fun when we were young — and they still are. Many of the classics, such as Twister, Scrabble, and the Game of Life, have been updated.

397. Check out current local member benefits on the AARP Now app or at memberoffers.aarp.org/entertainment. At press time in the Washington, DC, area, we found discounts on golf, dance lessons, kayaking, martial arts, bicycle rentals, roller skating, and more.

398. Visit AARP's Virtual Community Center at www.aarp.org/vcc for free interactive online events and classes such as line dancing, tai chi, and meditation. It's free for members and nonmembers.

Focusing on Fitness

Stay physically (and fiscally) fit with these money-saving tips from our experts, including classes, gym memberships, and sports equipment. And it's not just good for your body. Physical activity can boost memory, improve thinking, even lower the risk of dementia.

Saving on Gym Memberships and Training

399. If you prefer the community of in-person classes, most studios offer a free or highly discounted trial class or two. Once you've found one you love, consider buying a package of classes up front — as long as you're certain you'll use all the classes in the allotted time limit. Paying for six months' worth of classes at once is cheaper than paying for the classes as you go.

400. High demand for memberships from New Year's resolution-makers means that gyms tend to charge higher prices in January. You'll get a better deal in February. Or wait until summer, when membership rates — and prices — fall off.

401. Look for gym membership deals when you join with a friend or family member. Besides saving cash, you'll have an exercise buddy to keep you motivated.

402. Take advantage of discounted or even free gym memberships and training courses offered through your workplace benefits.

OLDER ADULTS

403. Join SilverSneakers. The program offers free gym memberships to people 65 and over. Save hundreds of dollars per year. Visit tools.silversneakers.com/ to see whether your health plan covers it and if you are eligible.

404. Consider small-group training. If you want a personal trainer, ask friends to join you. Many trainers offer money-saving training packages for small groups.

Exercising for Free (or Cheaply)

405. Whether you prefer gentle yoga, heart-pounding cardio, or sensible strengthening routines, you can find thousands of workout videos — available for free — online (one easy place to start is at aarp.org/fitness) or through some cable providers and streaming services. You don't need much for most of these workouts — just a yoga mat for floor exercise and enough space for a few steps (or lunges) in all directions around you.

406. Stream classes such as Daily Burn (dailyburn.com/), Crunch Live (www.crunchlive.com/), and YogaToday (www.yoga today.com/) for between $10 and $20 a month for unlimited access. That's the cost of one in-person class. And you decide when class starts.

407. Ask local retailers about free fitness classes. Nationwide chains like Lululemon, North Face, and REI offer free instructor-led workouts at select locations for a variety of activities.

408. Take advantage of free ways to exercise, such as walking, dancing, and stretching, or check out houses of worship and local YMCAs for exercise classes for little or no cost. Squeeze workouts into everyday activities, such as taking the stairs and parking farther from your destination, so you move more.

409. Perform body-weight exercise. These don't require equipment and can be done in small spaces, like your office. Examples include squats, lunges, jumping jacks, and crunches.

410. Join a health or nutrition challenge. Many free challenges are available online or in communities to help people get fit. Some provide online badges or other awards for motivation. Many employers also offer incentives for participation in exercise and other health programs.

411. For a fit body and mind in your 50s and beyond, regular exercise is key. Still, there are days when you just can't face the treadmill. Here are some ways to stay strong and limber when the gym is off the table.

- **Pull your stomach in.** To increase abdominal power without crunches, suck in your stomach. Stand straight, exhale, pull in your belly, and hold for 20 to 30 seconds (or as long as you can). Do three to five reps.

- **Clench those glutes.** You can build a stronger, less saggy butt by clenching those butt cheeks. This move works the gluteus maximus, gluteus medius, and gluteus minimus — a twerking trifecta. Stand, clench as tight as possible, and hold for 30 to 60 seconds. Start with three to five reps, gradually increasing the number over time. (If you clench your abs simultaneously, you'll strengthen your lower back; your glutes and abs help pull your pelvis into a powerful position.)

- **Circle your arms.** For shoulder power, extend your arms out, each to its respective side, and make ten small forward circles. Then make ten small backward circles. You'll probably feel a slight muscle burn. Next, try doing three to five reps forward and backward. This works your deltoids and rotator cuff muscles. Add in larger circles to increase your range of motion.

- **Sit up straight.** If you slump when you sit, this can lead to postural problems. Focus on sitting upright to strengthen your back and neck.

- **Use the stairs.** If you live or work in a building with a staircase, take advantage of it. You may not feel like hiking or jogging, but your quads still need to be worked. Even walking up just a couple of flights of stairs on a regular basis can help you develop power and stamina over the long run.

Saving on Sports Equipment

412. Looking to strength-train without spending hundreds of dollars on dumbbells? Purchasing a set of resistance bands is a cheap alternative and will still provide a full-body workout.

413. If you're interested in larger equipment, like a treadmill or stationary bike, check out sites such as Craigslist, Facebook Marketplace, and OfferUp, where your neighbors may be selling barely used equipment for much less than you'd pay at retail. A lot of people buy exercise equipment and don't use it. You can get little or never used equipment at a fraction of the cost.

414. While it's rarely necessary to purchase purpose-made workout clothing, new threads can give you some added motivation. The rewards programs at athletic apparel stores may give you access to exclusive deals and discounts on merchandise. Some stores, such as Athleta, Nike, and Reebok, may also provide access to community fitness events and classes.

415. When in doubt, go for inexpensive workout equipment. A jump rope, a pair of weights, and an exercise ball are cheap and effective.

Tech to Save You Money

416. With AARP Online Fitness powered by LIFT session, you can access free expert-led wellness webinars and fun 5- to 30- minute workouts, plus live and on demand classes, one-on-one training, and more. Once you subscribe, you can download the mobile app to access the program. AARP members save 50 percent off the annual subscription and 20 percent off personal coaching. Visit aarp.org/lift-session.

417. When it comes to fitness, like many endeavors, keeping track of what you plan to do, and when, has been shown to help people meet their goals. Apps can offer assistance in this area, whether they're counting your steps or charting your weekly strength-training goals.

Apps also offer something equally important, if less quantitative. Experts say people who use exercise apps have a lot more self-confidence in their ability to exercise, which itself leads to more exercise.

What's more, apps help remove barriers to exercise. These can be anything from insufficient motivation to lack of knowledge of how to exercise effectively. Research shows that the more barriers people have, the more likely they are to benefit from exercise apps.

If you're searching for a fitness app, know that many are free — though you may be required to look at the ads that come with them. To upgrade to an ad-free app, you usually have to pay a fee.

These four exercise apps — which are available for both iOS (iPhone) and Android — are easy to use and motivating:

- **Map My Fitness:** This all-in-one app tracks whatever workout you're doing: walking, biking, running, or swimming, as well as gym workouts, stair climbing, and strength training — including minutes and calories burned. If you're outdoors, it maps your route (and allows you to save your favorites). You can set goals for time, mileage (for everything from a few blocks to your first 5K or marathon), pace, and/or how many calories you want to burn. Guided training plans and audio coaching can help motivate you, step by step, to reach these goals. And because both are owned by Under Armour, your workouts can automatically link to MyFitnessPal, the popular fitness and diet tracker that's praised for nutrition features that let you drill down on specifics such as how much saturated fat or sodium you're taking in each day. (Map My Fitness, free; ad-free MVP membership, $5.99 per month; MyFitnessPal, free; ad-free MyFitnessPal Premium, $49.99 per year)

- **Runkeeper:** While most newer phones allow for free step counting, this app offers more options, including better accuracy and advanced graphics. It also offers optional audio updates during your workout and the ability to set your own personal goals, record your progress, and follow a tailor-made plan to help you improve your performance over time. Owned by sneaker company Asics, Runkeeper also lets you enter virtual races and join running/walking groups, as well as set reminders to get out and run or walk. (Free; $9.99 per month or $39.99 per year for Runkeeper Go premium upgrade)

- **Daily Workouts:** Tell this app how much time you have to exercise (5, 8, or 10 minutes) and select the body part you want to work (arms, butt, abs, or legs), and you'll get simple detailed exercises with videos for you to follow for your height, weight, age, and fitness level. (Daily Workouts Fitness Trainer, free; ad-free Daily Workouts Pro, $19.99)

  There's also a companion Simply Yoga app that uses audio to guide you through beginner through advanced poses for 20, 40, or 60 minutes. (Simply Yoga, free; ad-free Simply Yoga Pro, $14.99)

- **SilverSneakers Go:** The SilverSneakers health and fitness programs for adults 65 and up — covered by Medicare and offered at over 16,000 gyms nationwide — are now available in app form. Set workout schedules, find free SilverSneakers workout classes at gyms near you, and build 4- to 12-week workout programs — all geared to your fitness level (beginner, intermediate, or advanced). With strength, flexibility, cardio, and walking options, as well as specialized workouts for the lower back and hips, the app also provides the option of following a guided audio and/or video lesson while logging your workout activity, allowing you to measure your progress. Finally, the app will remind you — if you want — when it's time to exercise. And you may want to take it up on the offer; studies show that motivational messages within apps significantly up the overall time people report working out. (Free)

Having a Ball: Parties and Holidays

Holidays, birthdays, and get-togethers are special times to show people you care about them. But that doesn't mean you have to break the bank. Our experts have budget-conscious tips for parties, gifts, and celebrations that don't make you look like Scrooge.

Hosting Parties and Other Gatherings

418. Host morning parties. Brunch gatherings can be just as much fun as evening parties, and the foods you serve — such as egg dishes and savory and sweet breads — tend to be cheaper than what you serve for dinner. Plus, you likely won't go through as much wine.

419. Create a "cuisine club" with friends. The group selects a type of food for the evening's dinner — say, Greek, Thai, or Louisiana Creole — and then each person contributes a dish. It's less hassle for the host, and it's cheaper than a restaurant.

420. Instead of offering a full bar, serve wine and one specialty cocktail or punch. Give the cocktail or punch a fun name around the theme for your event.

421. Soup can be an inexpensive, fun, and unexpected hors d'oeuvre. Serve in small portions, in espresso cups or shot glasses.

422. Make edible centerpieces. This can be as simple as using a cluster of glasses or bowls for a display of veggies and hot dip.

423. Consider a stew for a dinner event. Stews let you take meat a lot further than as an individual menu item. Serve alongside a salad and homemade bread, and you have a wonderful, inexpensive meal option.

Enjoying Holidays and Birthdays on the Cheap

424. For Halloween and Christmas decorations, a neighborhood or backyard Easter egg hunt, and birthday celebrations, shop at discount and dollar stores. Holiday tchotchkes, gift wrap, cards, decorations, and party supplies of all kinds are cheap at Dollar General, Dollar Store, or Dollar Tree. (But note the prices — not all dollar stores keep prices to $1!) Sure, you may still spend more than you did a year ago for a bag of candy, but it's going to be a lot cheaper than it would cost at a drugstore or supermarket.

425. You can get 25 to 30 percent off chocolates, flowers, plants, fruit baskets, and gourmet food from FTD and Proflowers — great ways to show your appreciation or make your own home more festive. Visit aarp.org/flowers-gifts.

426. When held in check, holiday spending can be delightful, harmless fun, especially when you find the right gift for someone special. How do you keep your head and avoid blowing your budget? With careful thought, you can celebrate and be generous — without regret. Here are solutions to common holiday budget challenges.

- **Make a list — and check it twice. Challenge:** Right now, planning for the holidays seems overwhelming, and you're concerned about the cost. **Solution:** Create a complete holiday list before the big push starts.

Include all major items — gifts, food, and decorations for holiday parties, and festive clothing. Experts say that if you figure this out now, you'll be able to set a holiday budget far ahead of time, which will make it easier to stick to.

As you create this list, decide on the amount you can afford to spend on family members and friends, and stick to it. Resist the urge to buy something for everyone you know or to spend more than you've allotted.

- **Rethink Black Friday and Cyber Monday. Challenge:** There's tremendous pressure to buy on Black Friday and Cyber Monday, and it's hard to resist. **Solution:** Be strategic on those days — or let them pass you by.

Think back to the last Black Friday or Cyber Monday. Did you forget you were buying gifts and wind up with a pile of stuff for yourself that you couldn't resist?

True, with careful shopping you can get good deals on Black Friday and Cyber Monday. And other stores are likely to run related deals weeks beforehand. But if your impulse shopping tends to get out of hand, remind yourself that great deals can be had all year round. Think Presidents' Day, Mother's Day, Father's Day, Memorial Day, the Fourth of July, and Labor Day. Another example is Super Bowl Sunday. Rather than buying a TV on Cyber Monday, you may want to wait until late January. TV prices tend to drop just before the big game.

- **Buy in bulk when possible. Challenge:** You're hosting several parties at your home, and plan to attend more given by others. **Solution:** To please your guests and bring goodies to other hosts, look for opportunities to buy in bulk. For example, one case of your favorite moderately priced wine may cover multiple events. You can also find a wide assortment of festive foods at Costco or Sam's Club. Just be sure not to overbuy.

- **Just say no to some requests. Challenge:** There are too many celebrations to attend and too many pleas for donations. **Solution:** Feel free to decline the invitations to some parties and resist the temptation to buy a new outfit for the ones you accept.

Also, give yourself permission to scrutinize the charitable donations you're asked to make at work or in store checkout lines. Give if you like, but rather than contributing cash at the office or at the store, donate later by check or online. That way you can donate as much as you're comfortable with — without the pressure.

- **Ignore retail sales that look too good to be true. Challenge:** As the holidays get closer, many retailers boast sales of up to 70 percent off. **Solution:** If a retailer's holiday sale looks too good to be true, it probably is. Retailers often mark up the original price so high that 70 percent off is not nearly the bargain that it appears to be. These kinds of fat markups are particularly common at some department store chains. Instead, investigate how the 70 percent off pricing compares with other retailers.

- **Don't rush out to join a new membership club for the holidays. Challenge:** You have lots to buy, and new membership clubs offer holiday savings. **Solution:** Reevaluate the memberships you already have and double-check how you can best use them to save on holiday purchases. For example, all Amazon Prime members may not realize the early access they get to Prime deals that general shoppers don't get. And some "membership" clubs have no fees at all but can still offer shoppers some holiday budget relief. For example, the CVS loyalty card features ExtraBucks rewards for things you may purchase. For holiday shopping, first look for rewards or discounts like this that you may not be aware are sitting on.

427. It's understandable that you want to spoil the kids on Easter, adorning them with lavish baskets teeming with candy and other holiday treats. There's a reason the nation spends billions of dollars on Easter alone. A big way to save is to break that mold and rein in some of the spending and spoiling. The kids don't need it, and if it's too much it could end up being tossed, anyway. A box of chocolates, a gift card, or a morning spent decorating eggs together is a great way to celebrate without breaking the bank.

Giving Gifts

428. Give your time as a gift. Write out redeemable coupons for baby- and pet-sitting, free rides to someone who doesn't drive, or home-cooked meals.

429. AARP members receive a $110 voucher on their first order of $139.99 or more plus additional wine credits when they sign up to become a Naked Wines Angel. Visit aarp.org/naked-wines.

430. Price match with gusto. Many retailers — including Best Buy, Target, and Walmart — will often match the competition's prices when you present clear proof of a competitor's lower pricing. If you have a loyalty to one store but find a lower price at another, simply bring the proof of pricing, such as a printed ad, into the store you prefer, and there's a reasonably good chance that it will match it. But keep in mind that there's typically a strict window of time during which stores are willing to match competitor pricing, so make sure you're familiar with the time limits.

431. Make your own holiday or birthday gifts by making use of talents like painting, building, crafting, sewing, and card-making. Bake cookies or make jams, ornaments, or other craft items to give as presents. You can find items like baking supplies, jam jars, decorative bags, craft materials, and other items at discount and dollar stores. If you have kids or grandkids, involve them in the fun — you'll set a good example while creating a precious memory.

432. Instead of gifts for each member of a family, purchase a gift card the whole family can use for things like movies, bowling, or a ball game.

433. Offer to make dinner, give your partner a massage, deliver breakfast in bed, or take over a household chore. You can even find blank certificates online to fill in — "One massage," say, or "5 Sunday Breakfasts in Bed" — and stick in a card.

434. For small tokens for your hair stylist, building superintendent, or letter carrier, look to dollar stores, the Christmas Tree Shops, HomeGoods, or a similar discounter in your area.

435. Make a charitable donation in someone's name. Not only does it help you — and the receiver — feel better about doing good, but it also can help you save money in three ways. For one thing, those who receive the gift don't know the specific amount you sent — unless you tell them. They only know that a donation has been made in their name. So even relatively small donations can feel big. Second, charities offer things like T-shirts, socks, or a certificate to contributors so you have something that you can wrap up and send that memorializes the contribution. Third, you may also be able to take a tax deduction; talk with a tax expert.

436. Gifting gently used items sold online and at thrift stores — or available for free from your closet — is gaining popularity. Here are five acceptable secondhand gifts. Just be sure to never regift in the same friend circle. After all, you don't want to get caught.

- **Electronics and personal devices:** Smartphones, tablets, and computers are popular gifts to give during the holidays, but they can easily break the bank — unless you buy them refurbished. Many manufacturers and retailers sell refurbished electronics at a discounted rate.

  You have to be careful when going this route to ensure you get a device that's the correct model and in working condition. Experts say that the key to giving a used electronic is to make sure you're buying a certified refurbished option from a reputable retailer, which will come looking brand-new with an option for return and a warranty.

- **Toys for children:** Unless the children are super-savvy shoppers, they aren't likely to tell the difference between a new or used toy if it's in good condition. When you're buying a used toy, make sure to read the description for the wear and tear or look at it in person if you're buying through a local listing site to make sure it has all the parts needed.

- **Gift cards:** Gift cards tend to top holiday lists, yet many go unused each year. A CreditCards.com survey found 47 percent of U.S. adults said they have at least one unused gift card, store credit, or voucher adding up to $21 billion nationwide. If this sounds familiar, consider regifting one of your unused gift cards.

Don't have any? You can also save money by buying gift cards on a resale site. CardCash, GiftCash, Raise, and other sites sell unwanted gift cards and merchandise credits at a discount. The deal depends on the popularity of the gift card or brand.

Presentation goes a long way, so think about wrapping it in a mini gift bag or giving it with a corresponding token gift such as a candle to go with a massage certificate or a box of candy or popcorn to go with a movie theater gift card.

- **Housewares:** "One person's trash is another person's treasure" can be applied to gift giving if you're thoughtful about your selection. If you have an unused candle, coffee-table book, or cookie dish lying around that you know the recipient would love, pass it on.

- **Wine and liquor:** You can regift an unopened bottle of wine or liquor you know you won't drink but your friend will love. You save money, and you know it won't go to waste.

437. Don't wait until the last minute. Getting an early start on gift-buying will ultimately save you money, according to experts. Even though it may seem like an early start would result in spending more, it's a great way to avoid last-minute overspending and impulse buying. Some 27 percent of Gen Xers and 19 percent of boomers begin their holiday shopping before Halloween, which helps to spread out the cost of gift-giving over the course of the season, according to Klarna's 2021 "Holidays Unwrapped" report. Shopping this way also lets you take advantage of specials and deals. It's smart to keep track of the coming "deal" days for your favorite retailers (often advertised on their websites). Those may be the best times to shop online or in person at each of them.

438. Make a family decision on gift wrapping. Gift wrapping can be very expensive, particularly if you pay someone to do it for you. Limiting the amount of gift wrapping you do is an easy way to help stay within your holiday budget. For example, a family may decide to wrap gifts that will be opened together in town but not wrap gifts that are shipped to family who live out of town. The wrapping should not be done by professional gift wrappers or by retailers who charge for wrapped gifts, but by the family members themselves. Consider fun, homemade gift wrap, like the Sunday comics or hand-decorated paper. Also, decorative holiday gift bags are a great option for gift wrap because they can be reused.

439. Shop with cash only. Shopping with cash for the holidays may sound unfriendly in a highly digital world. But think of it this way: If your budget is $100 and you put $100 in your wallet to spend for all your holiday gifts, you will absolutely know when you've reached your maximum. Some experts also recommend keeping your cash in larger bills because most shoppers are more reluctant to frivolously spend them.

Tech to Save You Money

440. Verify online that every deal is the best. The very smartest holiday shoppers always confirm that they are getting the absolute best deal before buying, whether online or in person. If you don't verify pricing online, you're almost certain to be paying more than you need to. Check all major retail websites and search the shopping tab in your browser. You never know where the best deals will be.

441. Nab additional savings at sites like Capital One Shopping, CouponCabin.com, and RetailMeNot.com. Consider downloading the browser extensions of these sites and the deals will pop up automatically.

Providing for Your Pets

| f you have a pet, you want to give it the best care possible. That may be harder to afford right now, with prices rising on everything from dog food to cat litter. But you can still afford a pet with these expert tips.

Adopting and Taking Care of a Pet

442. Adopt a rescue pet. Even if the rescue organization or shelter charges a small fee, your furry friend will be cheaper than from a breeder and healthier and better adjusted than from a puppy mill. Rescue animals usually come spayed or neutered, vaccinated, microchipped, and protected against ticks, fleas, and heartworm disease. And no small thing: You're saving a life.

OLDER ADULTS

443. Nonprofit Pets for the Elderly helps people 60 and older with reduced-price pet adoption from 56 shelters located in 35 states. And some shelters offer help with medical bills, food, and other pet needs instead of an adoption discount. Visit www.petsfortheelderly.org.

444. Go to HumaneSociety.org for a list of programs offering assistance with pet expenses. Search "affording your pet" on the site.

445. Groom your own pet. You'll save money — groomers charge for clipping nails, haircuts, and bathing — as well as the hassle of making an appointment and the time to go there. Find out how to do it yourself — YouTube has instructions for many breeds.

446. Maintain a regular dental routine. Dental and periodontal problems in pets can lead to serious — and expensive — illnesses, including heart and kidney disease. Ask your vet which products to use and how often, including pet-safe toothpaste and Greenies or Milk-Bone Brushing Chews to remove plaque.

447. Try a pet food subscription or in-store loyalty card. Both can nab you lower prices on your furry friend's everyday chow. A subscription could save you 5 percent on each order, often with free delivery and, in some cases, a 30 to 35 percent discount on your first order. Most stores let you change or cancel your subscription at any time. Some pet stores offer in-store programs like "buy three, get one free" for pet food, too.

448. Invest in toys that will survive your pet's most rigorous workout. Some toys can last a pet's lifetime. Check out toys by Kong or Orbee, or knock-off brands for similar items.

449. The Society for Human Resource Management reports that just 7 percent of employers allow pets in the workplace. Surcharges at so-called pet-friendly hotels can range from $30 to $90 per night. If you fly, be prepared to pay as much as $100 per pet carrier in the cabin, or $200 if you check your pet as baggage — which would be highly stressful.

So how can you provide affordable, loving care while you are gone? Professional pet services can be pricey. Devising the best and most cost-effective solution starts with determining how much alone time your pet can tolerate without undue stress or behavioral issues, as well as figuring out what resources are readily available.

- **Tailor their daytime care to their schedules.** Your pet may not need as much attention during the day as you think. Adult dogs need 12 to 14 hours of sleep a day and are typically active for just 4 or 5 hours. Cats can sleep 16 to 20 hours a day and tend to be more active at dawn and dusk. Don't spend money on full-time daycare if all they need is a quick trip outside.

People often think of cats as easier; they seem to enjoy their solitude more than dogs, and a litter box eliminates the need to walk them. But the notion that all felines are independent is a misconception. Experts recommend looking for changes in your cat's habits after it has spent time alone. Play biting, pouncing, excessive vocalizing, or destructive behavior may be signs that your cat isn't getting enough from you or its environment. Age is also a consideration. Young cats and kittens, who need more attention, will be calmer and more well-behaved if they don't spend hours alone. Seniors can be more sensitive to routine changes than others.

Likewise, a dog's tolerance for solitude depends on its personality. Signs of anxiety include nervous pacing and panting and changes in posture and body language, which can include tenseness, a low tail, ears back, a furrowed brow, wide eyes, trembling, whining, or trying to leave with you as you prepare to depart. Most healthy dogs can hold their bladder for up to eight hours or longer, but letting them out at least every six hours is better — and less risky for your rugs.

- **Ease them into new schedules.** Most animals don't like a sudden change in their schedule, and if you suddenly disappear for eight hours each day, you'll simply make them more anxious. To acclimate your cat or dog to change, experts recommend that you slowly adjust things. This way, your pet can begin getting used to a new walking, feeding, napping, and playing schedule.

Practice giving your pet longer periods of solitude, with soothing music or the TV in the background, while you go to the store or do yard work. Offer healthy chews or toys stuffed with favorite foods that have been frozen, such as peanut butter, canned pet food, plain yogurt, or low-fat cottage cheese. Likewise, give your cat toys and cardboard boxes to play with or scratching posts to use. These are low-cost ways of keeping your pet calmer if you are delayed for some reason.

- **Pet doors can save money.** If you have a fenced-in yard, you may want to consider a pet door, which can save you the cost of hiring a dog walker. HomeAdvisor.com estimates the cost of buying and installing a cat door to be between $75 and $400. A typical range for a dog door is $100 to $2,000. The best ones are airtight and tamper-proof and have a lock system. You should also look for a door that only opens with a microchip on your pet's collar; otherwise, that adorable raccoon could follow your pet inside. Make sure your favorite friends are current on all vaccines and can't jump over or tunnel under the fence. And never leave pets unattended for long.

A pet door may not work for all dogs. For example, if your pet is particularly terrified of thunder or other loud noises, a door may not be a good solution. You should also be sure that your fence is secure enough to prevent other animals — such as foxes and coyotes — from getting into your yard.

- **Ask friends, family, or neighbors to visit.** They can walk them or let them out, break up the day, and reduce their sense of isolation when you're away. If you know other cat or dog lovers in your building or down the street, you can take turns making lunchtime visits. The goal is to arrange pet visits or have your pet stay in their home when you work or travel, and vice versa.

Vetstreet.com, which offers advice from veterinarians, suggests having someone your cat knows well check in daily if you will be gone more than 24 hours. That's true even if you leave provisions for a longer period. Have your visitor provide fresh food and water and scoop out the litter box.

- **Shop carefully for paid caregivers.** If you must pay for services, then ask your veterinarian, dog trainer, animal shelter, or neighbors for recommendations. Pet sitters cost, on average, about $25 for 30 minutes or $75 to $85 per night.

Cheaper is not necessarily better, but it's a good idea to get several bids. Narrow your choices to one or two people you have properly screened and evaluated and whom you can use consistently. Pets with underlying behavior issues, such as anxiety or fear, do much better with caregivers they know and have come to trust than with a series of strangers, experts say.

When choosing a walker, sitter, or daycare provider (assuming your dog enjoys playing with others), consider how much attention your pets require based on their energy level, desire for human contact, potty schedule, and medical needs. And whomever you choose, do a background check. Some apps require them for caregivers. Some, but not all, dog walkers and pet sitters are insured and bonded, or have backing from a local vet. Insist on references from previous clients and plan a walk to see how the person handles your dog. As you would with a babysitter, provide your contact information, specific instructions, the phone numbers and addresses of your local and emergency vets, and how you want the person to respond should certain situations arise.

- **For challenging issues, stick with the pros.** If your dog or cat has serious issues (high stress or aggression, for example, or a serious medical condition), contact a trainer or behavior consultant, who can offer tips and tricks for helping your four-legged friend adjust to a new routine. The cost, the ASPCA estimates, will be about $200 per hour. It's better to identify problems and treat them early, rather than waiting to see if they get worse. Generally, it's harder to treat separation anxiety than prevent it. The ASPCA has information on how to get treatment for a difficult pet. Putting off treatment will only make it more difficult for your pet and more expensive for you.

450. Ask about pet food and services at food banks. Your local community may offer resources that help cover costs. During the pandemic, the ASPCA began distributing food for dogs and cats through regular food banks to take advantage of the distribution infrastructure that was already in place. It offers such services in New York City, Los Angeles, and Miami, as well as in Oklahoma for horses and other equines. Pet owners are encouraged to contact their local food banks and animal shelters to find out more about what resources, including pet food, supplies, and/or medical care, may be available.

Other nonprofits are also ready to help, as they strive to help people keep their animals rather than having to surrender them to a shelter. GOODS, a program of the Seattle, Washington–based Greater Good Charities, distributes pet food and supplies to animal rescue partners in the United States and abroad. It sources and manages excess, rebranded, and short-dated food and supplies from donors, including manufacturers, distributors, and retailers. GOODS then makes them available to thousands of animal welfare organizations, food banks, Veteran Affairs locations, and other qualified agencies.

Visiting the Vet and Getting Pet Health Insurance

451. Ask if pet prescriptions can be filled at your local human pharmacy. And consider GoodRx and RxSaver, pharmacy discount websites for human medications, which may also offer the brand-name or generic medications your pet needs. GoodRx offers coupons for savings on some pet drugs at www.goodrx.com/pets.

452. Check with your vet about generic pet meds. As with human medications, generic pet drugs cost less than brand-name ones.

453. Consider whether pet health insurance may be right for you and your pets. The ASPCA recommends that if you want it, purchase coverage while your pet is healthy. Whether insurance is worth it is up to you. In a Forbes Advisor survey, nearly eight in ten pet owners said they don't have pet insurance. And their choice wasn't necessarily related to income level. Some pet owners decide that the coverage isn't worth the cost of the premiums paid.

454. Save 10 percent on monthly premiums for pet insurance with Fetch by The Dodo. Plans cover qualifying care for injuries and illnesses, emergency vet visits, prescription medications and supplements, plus boarding fees should your pet require hospitalization. Visit aarp.org/pet-insurance.

455. Think "preventive care." Regard your pet's health as you do your own. Preventive healthcare can help stave off a long list of health problems and diseases. And while preventive care has its costs, it saves you money in the long run. The ASPCA offers some advice here.

- **Schedule your pet's annual exam.** It's much more expensive to treat illnesses than protect against them.

- **Protect your pet with vaccines.** Some vaccines are optional, while others are essential to prevent serious diseases. Discuss your pet's particular needs with your vet. Some areas have clinics that will vaccinate your pet at cost or for free, and your veterinarian may offer a payment plan if you can't afford vaccinations.

- **Prevent fleas and ticks.** They can cause minor skin irritations as well as life-threatening blood loss and disease. Use topical flea and tick solutions as directed, never substituting a product intended for a dog on a cat, or vice versa.

- **Watch your dog's skin.** Excessive scratching, chewing, and licking may indicate external parasites, infections, allergies, metabolic problems, and stress, or a combination of these.

456. Shop for vet services before you need them. If free services are limited or unavailable in your area, then shop veterinary practices, comparing fees and costs, before an emergency occurs. Should illness strike, talk with the vet and choose the treatment plan that matches your goals and available resources.

Tech to Save You Money

457. Consider expanding your support system by using apps such as Rover, Thumbtack, and Wag!, which feature a range of services. These apps connect you with qualified pet sitters and walkers in your area. Nearly all of them offer reviews, background checks, and pet insurance.

For instance, Rover is an online platform that allows you to connect with pet sitters in your area. First, check the sitters' reviews and pick your favorite. You can then schedule a meet and greet. Once you book, your reservation comes with 24/7 support, pet health insurance, and oftentimes photo and video updates. Thumbtack, too, offers pet sitters. Depending on which app you use, you can also choose how long you want them to spend with your pet each day. Some sites offer everything from drop-in visits to house-sitting to boarding.

If you just need a walker, check out apps like Wag! This app allows you to pick a trusted and reviewed walker in your area. It's a nifty way to give your pets the exercise they need while you're relaxing on your trip.

458. Review airlines' pet policies on BringFido.com (www.bringfido.com/travel/), PetFriendlyTravel.com (petfriendlytravel.com/pet-air-travel/), and PetTravel.com (www.pettravel.com/airline_rules.cfm), which have compiled the major airlines' policies. Policies can vary considerably, whether they're about weight restrictions, fees, or acceptable carrier sizes. Most airlines require pet carriers to fit under the seat in front of you — that's a pretty small space. The carrier will be counted as your one carry-on item. On Qatar Airways, you can bring only falcons and in certain cases service animals onboard.

Turning Your Personal Finances Around

ind ways to cut home, auto, and life insurance costs and credit card debt, plus how to budget wisely and protect your assets. Here, AARP experts offer their ideas to sharpen your money management skills.

Saving on Home, Auto, and Life Insurance

459. Ask about safe homeownership discounts. If you've gone a long time without making a claim, your home insurance company may discount premiums by as much as 20 percent.

460. Installing "smart" home devices — like video doorbells, smart smoke detectors, and water leak sensors — could lower your home insurance premium by up to 15 percent, depending on the insurance company. Just having a fire extinguisher can lower your home insurance premium by 5 percent.

461. Raise your deductible. An increase from $500 to $1,000 can save you up to 25 percent on a homeowner's premium.

462. Companies charge up to 20 percent less if you get both home and auto insurance policies from them.

STUDENTS

463. Get the good-student discount. If your teen gets good grades, you could get an average annual auto insurance discount of several hundred dollars.

464. Reduce your auto insurance. As your car ages, the maximum payout for an accident (calculated by subtracting your deductible from the car's value) steadily decreases. Crunch the numbers to see if the price of collision and comprehensive coverage is still worth it.

OLDER ADULTS

465. Refreshing your driving skills can improve your safety while reducing your auto insurance costs. Take the AARP Smart Driver online course to see how much you can save on multiyear car insurance bills. Visit www.aarp.org/driversafety. Please consult your insurance agent for applicability in your state.

466. AARP members have access to vehicle, homeowners, and renters insurance from the AARP Auto & Home Insurance Program from The Hartford. Enter or mention your AARP membership number to get a quote online or by phone. Members can get exclusive savings off their premiums, plus discounts for requesting a quote online or for bundling auto and home policies. Visit aarp.org/insurance-benefits.

467. Some insurers offer discounts if you prove that you drive safely by using a device for your car that measures your driving, including your rate of acceleration and breaking. Nationwide insurance, for example, offers a SmartRide discount of up to 40 percent, or up to $400 off a $1,000 policy.

468. People who exercise, maintain a healthy weight, and don't smoke can get as much as a 50 percent savings on life insurance.

469. Life insurers have price breaks at certain amounts, called *price bands*. When you move up a band, the cost per thousand dollars of coverage goes down. If you're looking at a $450,000 policy, get a price quote for $500,000 — it may be cheaper for more coverage.

470. You can apply for exclusive life insurance from AARP Life Insurance Options from New York Life. Specially trained agents can help evaluate your needs and explore insurance solutions. Find out more at aarp.org/life-insurance or call 800-793-1296.

Paying Less on Credit Cards —
or Letting Them Pay You

471. Assuming you pay your bill each month, choose cards that pay you, either in points, cash back, or travel rewards. You can maximize rewards by using several cards and dedicating each to its best purposes — say one gives you 5 percent cash back on gas while another gives you 5 percent on groceries. How many cards? Three or four at most. You don't want so many that you lose track of the bills; forgetting just one payment can unleash enough penalties and interest to wipe out a year of rewards. Card companies change terms constantly, so research online for the best cards for you and your family. And be sure to use your credit card points before they lose value. Don't waste the cash or credits!

Member Benefits AARP

472. The AARP Essential Rewards Mastercard from Barclays offers 3 percent cash back on gas station and drugstore purchases (excluding Target and Walmart), 2 percent cash back on medical expenses, and 1 percent cash back on all other purchases. There's no annual fee. Upon approval, cardmembers can earn a $100 cash-back bonus if they spend $500 in the first three months. Visit aarp.org/barclays-card.

473. Carrying credit card debt? You're not alone. Total credit card debt now stands at $890 billion, according to the Federal Reserve Bank of New York.

If you pay your balances off monthly, then the Federal Reserve's interest rate increases shouldn't concern you. If you carry a balance on your credit card, however, the Fed's rate hikes are particularly bad news. Higher rates mean that consumers and businesses pay more in interest, and that reduces their ability to spend.

What does the Fed's short-term interest rate have to do with your credit card? Most credit card rates are variable, meaning they can go up and down, and they're based on what's called the *prime rate,* which typically sits 3 percentage points above the federal funds rate. Banks usually raise their prime rates within 24 hours after the Fed announces an increase in the federal funds rate.

The prime rate is just a starting point for credit card rates: No one pays the prime rate on a credit card. Typically, banks add 10 percentage points or more to the prime rate and then tailor their credit card rates to a customer's credit rating. For example, a credit card's interest rate, known as the annual percentage rate (APR), may be 11 percentage points above the prime rate for customers with an excellent credit rating, and 20 percentage points for customers with an okay rating.

If you're carrying credit card balances, what should you do?

- **Pay them off as quickly as you can to avoid mounting interest.** Credit cards charge interest daily. If you have a $5,000 balance and pay $121 every other week rather than $242 at the end of the month, Bankrate.com says you can cut interest payments by $359 a year on a card with a 17 percent interest rate.

- **Get a new card.** Experts say that if you have good credit, you should grab one of the 0 percent introductory offers. Some offers give you as long as 21 months, at zero interest, to get that debt paid off. That's a great way to pay down your debt. Say you had $5,000 in credit card debt, and your interest rate was 17 percent. Payment: $250. You'd save about $900 in interest with a 0 percent rate card and, assuming you continued to pay $250 a month, you'd pay off the bill in 20 months. And after that, you'd have an extra $250 a month in your bank account.

- **Shop around for a lower interest rate.** If you can't get a zero-interest card, look for a card with a lower rate, or consider asking your current card issuer if it would consider giving you a lower rate. Although you may expect a hollow chuckle from the customer service rep, consumers who asked for a waiver or reduction on their annual fees had a 9-in-10 chance of success, according to a LendingTree study.

- **Apply for a personal loan.** You can still get personal loans with rates in the single digits, experts say. If you pay off your credit card with a personal loan, put your credit card aside and pay for things with cash (or charge only what you can afford to repay each month, so interest doesn't accrue). Otherwise, you'll end up with a big credit-card bill as well as a personal loan payment.

- **Ride the avalanche.** If you have several credit cards you want to pay off, try the avalanche method: making the minimum monthly payments on all of your credit cards and putting any surplus cash you have toward paying down your card with the highest interest rate. When that highest-rate card is paid off, target the one with the next-highest rate until all your debt is paid off. This method minimizes the overall amount of interest you're paying.

- **Make a snowball.** The snowball method takes a different tack than the avalanche method. The snowball method focuses on paying off the card with the lowest balance first, regardless of interest rate. Once that card is paid off, put your surplus cash toward paying off the next low-balance card you hold. It's not as efficient as the avalanche method, but paying off that first card quickly is a nice psychological boost that increases the likelihood of sticking to your debt-repayment goals.

If none of these strategies work for you, and you feel that you're continually sinking deeper into debt, consider seeing a credit counselor, who can help you set up a budget and talk to your creditors about payment plans. You can find a nonprofit credit counseling agency through the National Foundation for Credit Counseling (www.nfcc.org/). NFCC members are 501(c)3 charities and must meet accreditation standards and offer financial literacy programs in addition to debt management.

Getting Help with Mortgages

474. Did you get nailed with a late fee because you paid your mortgage a few days late? Call to waive late fees. Unless you're chronically late, they'll almost surely waive the fee if you ask.

475. A 30-year, $300,000 mortgage at 4 percent costs $1,432 a month. But if you pay $716 every two weeks instead, you can cut interest payments by $34,000 over the life of the loan.

476. Many states offer property tax breaks for homeowners over 65, including rebates, caps on assessed value, and tax-rate or assessment freezes. Such breaks could easily save you thousands of dollars a year. Visit ptaconsumers.aarp foundation.org/ for help with property taxes.

OLDER ADULTS

Keeping More of Your Money

477. Get taxes done free. AARP Foundation Tax-Aide offers in-person and virtual free tax preparation, with a focus on taxpayers who are 50+ with low to moderate incomes. Tax-Aide volunteers are located nationwide and are trained and IRS-certified every year to make sure they know about and understand the latest changes and additions to the tax code. Go to aarp.org/taxaide or call 888-687-2277.

478. Create a target savings rate. Diverting 10 percent of monthly income to savings and 10 percent to retirement investments is a good rule of thumb.

479. Challenge yourself to a no-spend month when you forbid any nonessential purchases. Feel like a month is too much to handle? Try declaring one day each week a "no-spend day."

480. Pay yourself. Put an open jar in a conspicuous place in your home. When you do something you might have paid for — ironing, cooking, fixing a good latte — feed the jar with the amount you'd have spent. Do the same if you resist the impulse to buy something. Watch the money add up, fast.

481. Negotiate all your bills. Almost every bill is at least slightly negotiable. Call your credit card, gym, cable, streaming service, newspaper, car insurance, internet, and phone companies once a year to remind them what a good customer you are, and ask what they're able to do to keep you.

482. Use a digital-only bank. It offers better savings rates. Say the average annual percentage yield (APY) on savings accounts is around 0.08 percent, but online banks offer APYs around 1.5 percent. If you stash $20,000 for a year, for example, the earning difference will be $286.

483. Get reimbursed for ATM fees. Most online banks and some traditional banks will reimburse you for fees incurred when you use another bank's ATM. But you have to ask.

OLDER ADULTS

484. Every year, Americans leave more than $16 billion in government benefits they're qualified for on the table. BenefitsCheckUp (benefitscheckup.org), the National Council on Aging's free online tool, can link you with benefits programs that can help pay for healthcare, medicine, food, utilities, and more.

Tech to Save You Money

485. Protect your identity — and your money — with AARP Identity Theft Protection powered by Norton. Members save up to 53 percent on plans that help protect against hackers stealing their personal information and infecting their devices with malware. Options for individuals, couples, and families are available. Terms apply. Visit aarp.org/norton-identity-theft or call 844-506-4198.

486. Apps such as Acorns, Albert, and Digit help build savings in small increments. Some round up your purchases to the nearest dollar and put the change in savings. Others analyze your checking daily and transfer money to savings.

OLDER ADULTS

487. The National Council on Aging has created a special online budget checkup tool for older adults called the AgeWellPlanner. It's specifically designed for people 65 and older who don't know how to create an annual budget.

488. Plan next month's spending. Budgeting apps like Mint, NerdWallet, Rocket Money, and You Need a Budget can help users focus on where their money should go in the coming weeks, not just where it went last month, help track your finances, and alert you when your bills are due.

489. Check out AARP Money Map, a free online tool that helps you save for emergencies or large purchases and learn new ways that budgeting can turn your goals into reality. Visit www.aarp.org/moneymap. No membership required.

Investing for the Long Term

When considering investment advice, keep in mind that your financial situation is unique. The tips our experts offer here may suit your circumstances, but if you have questions, you may want to consult an expert.

Finding the Right Advisor

490. Just as there's a medical specialist for most every ailment, there's a financial specialist for most every money-related problem or need. The Financial Industry Regulatory Authority (FINRA), Wall Street's self-regulatory organization, lists 212 different credentials or designations, ranging from AAI (accredited advisor in insurance) to WMS (wealth management specialist). All those abbreviations can confuse more than inform. Bottom line: You want someone who can help you protect and grow your money.

When the time comes to seek professional help to rethink investments, plan retirement finances, deal with debt, or take on any other money-related task, your first move is to find the right expert. How?

Check that the advisor is permitted to sell securities or give investment advice and has a clean record. Visit broker check.finra.org or call FINRA at 800-289-9999. Insurance sellers need a state license.

If the advisor uses a title, find out who awarded it and what it required. Some titles take little effort to obtain. FINRA has a directory of designations at www.finra.org/investors/professional-designations.

Watch for red flags when you first meet, such as promises of above-market returns or risk-free investing, a hard sell on certain products, or failure to ask about your specific financial needs and goals.

For help in finding a financial advisor, use AARP's Interview an Advisor tool at www.aarp.org/interviewanadvisor.

Making the Most of Your Investments

491. Keeping investing costs low is one of the most important things you can do to boost your returns. That's why index funds are good. What's more, Standard & Poor's research indicates that over time, index funds consistently outperform actively managed accounts.

492. Buy mutual funds, not stocks. Have both stock funds and bond funds in your portfolio to balance growth and safety.

493. If you've got some old dogs — investment losers, that is — sitting in your portfolio, selling them for a loss could provide a tax benefit.

494. If you're confused and intimidated by the prospect of investing, buy a target-date retirement fund. These funds are a simple way to own a diversified portfolio of stocks and bonds that gradually gets more conservative as you near retirement. Choose funds with low fees. You can find low-fee choices at major brokerages including Fidelity, Schwab, T. Rowe Price, and Vanguard, or do some comparison shopping at www.morningstar.com/target-date-funds.

495. The phone rings, and a friendly, energetic-sounding stranger is on the line asking if you have a minute to discover how to triple your money in just six months by investing in gold and silver mines. Or maybe you get an email urging you to buy shares of a company whose stock price is sure to go through the roof. It sounds too good to be true — because it *is* too good to be true.

Each year, fraud siphons billions from investors, according to the North American Securities Administrators Association. This isn't new. In the early 1920s, to name one famous example, a con artist named Charles Ponzi fleeced scores of Americans by promising lavish returns from a strange scheme to speculate in international coupons used by people in different countries to send each other return postage. In reality, Ponzi was using new investors' money to pay off existing investors.

It's a trick that criminals still employ. But in today's world, they have more — and more powerful — ways to reach ordinary people (robocalls, email, TV, social media) and convince them to hand over their money.

Fraud criminals target people of all ages, education and socioeconomic levels, gender, and racial/ethnic backgrounds with phony investment schemes. Watch for the following warning signs:

- A caller who pressures you to send money right away to take advantage of a supposedly once-in-a-lifetime opportunity.

- A caller who uses phrases such as "incredible gains," "breakout stock pick," or "huge upside and almost no risk!" The U.S. Securities and Exchange Commission (SEC) says such claims suggest high risk and possible fraud.

- Recommendations of foreign or "offshore" investments from someone you don't already know and trust. Once your money is in another country, the SEC cautions, it's more difficult to keep watch over it.

Protect yourself with these do's and don'ts:

- Do ask plenty of questions before you make any investment, including the following: Is the financial product registered with the SEC or state securities agencies? What are the fees? How does the investment company make money? What factors could affect the value of the investment?

- Do your homework. If you're considering investing in a publicly traded company, look up information about its finances and operations in the SEC's EDGAR database (www.sec.gov/edgar/searchedgar/companysearch).

- Do get advice from a person you trust and respect before making any decisions.

- Do know who's handling your investment. Conduct a background search in BrokerCheck, an online database maintained by FINRA. Visit brokercheck.finra.org/.

- Do be wary of free investment seminars, especially ones that include free meals. The SEC says scammers often figure that if they do you a small favor, you'll feel obligated to invest.

- Do have an exit strategy. FINRA recommends rehearsing some stock lines to cut short a caller's high-pressure pitch, such as "I'm sorry, I'm not interested. Thank you."

- Don't make investment decisions based on ads, TV commercials, phone calls, or email solicitations.

- Don't get dollar signs in your eyes. Con artists like to dangle the prospect of fabulous wealth to distract you from realizing the whole thing is a scam.

- Don't jump on "inside" information posted to social media, chat rooms, or forums promoting shares of a company that are certain to go up. It may be a "pump-and-dump" — a ploy to drive up the price artificially, enabling scammers to sell their shares for a big profit before the stock crashes and the remaining investors take a loss.

- Don't believe someone claiming to represent FINRA who offers an investment guarantee — the organization says its officers and employees never do this. Some particularly audacious scammers pose as FINRA executives to create a false sense of security about an investment and secure an advance fee.

- Don't judge an investment opportunity by a company's professional-looking website. These days, crooks can easily create a convincing online facade.

- Don't make an immediate impulse-buying decision. Wait at least 24 hours to allow emotions to subside before making a purchase.

Participating in Retirement Accounts

496. Invest in your company's retirement accounts, such as a 401(k), a 403(b), or, for federal workers, a Thrift Savings Plan. Your employer will deduct your pretax contributions from your paycheck, and your savings will be tax-deferred until you take withdrawals during retirement. (The exception is Roth accounts, which are funded with after-tax dollars and from which withdrawals in retirement are tax-free.) As of 2023, the contribution limit is $22,500, or for people aged 50-plus, $30,000.

If you can't afford to contribute the maximum, invest what you can and then try to increase that amount each year. You may find that putting pretax money into your account doesn't affect your paycheck as much as you'd think, because of the tax savings.

497. Contribute enough to take advantage of your employer's match. Many employers automatically match a percentage of your contributions, which is essentially free money and can make a big difference in the amount of money in your account at retirement.

Say you're 50 years old and you earn $50,000, you put 5 percent of your salary a year into your 401(k), and you get 3 percent raises each year until you retire at 65. You'll have $87,376 in your account when you retire, factoring in a 7 percent annual rate of return. Now say your employer matches 50 percent of your contribution up to 5 percent of your salary. You'll have $131,064 in your account, according to AARP's 401(k) calculator. Visit www.aarp.org/work/retirement-planning/401k_calculator.html.

498. Consider tax diversification in your retirement account. Many plans have added Roth options — which allow you to contribute dollars you've already paid taxes on and then withdraw the money in retirement tax free. If you think your tax bracket will go up in the future, stashing some contributions here can be smart.

Tech to Save You Money

499. Use AARP's free online tools to estimate your income taxes, find out how to maximize your Social Security benefits, see whether you're saving enough for retirement, and more. Visit www.aarp.org/tools.

500. Use FINRA's fund analyzer to check the fees in your mutual funds and compare the costs. Just a 1 percent annual fee on investments can cost you thousands by the time you retire. Visit tools.finra.org/fund_analyzer.

Index

Y

Publisher's Acknowledgments

Senior Acquisitions Editor:
Tracy Boggier

Senior Managing Editor:
Kristie Pyles

Compilation Editor:
Georgette Beatty

Development Editor: Linda Brandon

Copy Editor: Christine Pingleton

AARP Books Director: Jodi Lipson

Proofreader: Debbye Butler

Production Editor:
Tamilmani Varadharaj

Cover Images: © Getty Images